# Brain Games

# Brain Games

A supplement to
Childcraft—The How and Why Library

World Book, Inc.
a Scott Fetzer company
Chicago
www.worldbook.com

# Staff

## Executive Committee

**President**
Paul A. Gazzolo

**Vice President and Chief Financial Officer**
Donald D. Keller

**Vice President and Editor in Chief**
Paul A. Kobasa

**Vice President and Chief Marketing Officer**
Patricia Ginnis

**Vice President, Licensing & Business Development**
Richard Flower

**Chief Technology Officer**
Tim Hardy

**Managing Director, International**
Benjamin Hinton

**Director, Human Resources**
Bev Ecker

## Editorial

**Associate Director, Supplementary Publications**
Scott Thomas

**Managing Editor, Supplementary Publications**
Barbara A. Mayes

**Manager, Contracts & Compliance (Rights & Permissions)**
Loranne K. Shields

**Senior Editor**
Kristina Vaicikonis

**Administrative Assistant**
Ethel Matthews

## Graphics and Design

**Manager**
Tom Evans

**Coordinator, Design Development and Production**
Brenda B. Tropinski

**Associate Designer**
Matt Carrington

## Production

**Director, Manufacturing and Pre-Press**
Carma Fazio

**Manufacturing Manager**
Steven K. Hueppchen

**Production/ Technology Manager**
Anne Fritzinger

**Manuscript Production Specialist**
Curley Hunter

**Proofreader**
Emilie Schrage

## Marketing

**Director, Direct Marketing**
Mark R. Willy

**Marketing Analyst**
Zofia Kulik

For information about other World Book publications, visit our Web site at **www.worldbook.com** or call **1-800-WORLDBK (967-5325)**. For information about sales to schools and libraries, call **1-800-975-3250 (United States)**, or **1-800-837-5365 (Canada)**.

© 2010 World Book, Inc. All rights reserved. This volume may not be reproduced in whole or in part in any form without prior written permission from the publisher.

CHILDCRAFT, CHILDCRAFT—THE HOW AND WHY LIBRARY, and the GLOBE DEVICE are registered trademarks or trademarks of World Book, Inc.

World Book, Inc.
233 N. Michigan Ave.
Chicago, IL 60601

Printed in the United States of America by RR Donnelley, Willard, Ohio

1st printing April 2010

**Library of Congress Cataloging-in-Publication Data**

Brain games : a supplement to Childcraft—the how and why library.
   p. cm.
   Summary: "A collection of mazes, riddles from around the world, a mystery story, and picture, word, logic, number, and matchstick puzzles"--Provided by publisher.
   ISBN 978-0-7166-0624-6
   1. Puzzles--Juvenile literature. 2. Games--Juvenile literature.
I. World Book, Inc. II. Childcraft.
GV1493.B6732 2010
793.73--dc22
                                              2010000781

# Contents

# Acknowledgments

Sudoku puzzles (pp. 178-181) from *Kids' Sudoku For Dummies* by Andrew Heron. Copyright © 2007, Wiley Publishing. Reproduced with permission of John Wiley & Sons, Inc.

KenKen® puzzles (pp. 182-185) from *Will Shortz Presents I Can KENKEN! Volume 3* by Tetsuya Miyamoto. Published by St. Martins Press. Copyright © 2008, KenKen Puzzle LLC. KenKen® is a registered trademark of Nextoy. All rights reserved. By permission of Nextoy, LLC.

## Illustration Acknowledgments

The publishers of Childcraft gratefully acknowledge the courtesy of the following individuals and agencies for illustrations in this volume. When all the illustrations for a sequence of pages are from a single source, the inclusive page numbers are given. Credits should be read left to right, top to bottom, on their respective pages. All illustrations are the exclusive property of the publishers of Childcraft.

### Covers
Aristocrat, Discovery, International, and Standard Bindings: Daniel Krall
Heritage Binding: George Suyeoka, Yoshi Miyake, Diane Paterson, Christine di Monda, Kathy Clo, Heidi Palmer, Jan Jones
Rainbow Binding: © Shutterstock; © Jordi Caprí / Alamy

### Illustrations
10-11: Robert Byrd
12-13: Jan Jones
14-15: Dennis Hockerman
16: Jan Jones
17-19: Robert Byrd
20-21: Jan Jones
22-23: Robert Byrd
24-25: Robert Byrd; Dennis Hockerman
26-27: Dennis Hockerman; Robert Byrd
28-29: Robert Byrd; Jan Jones; Dennis Hockerman
30-31: Jan Jones; Robert Byrd
34: Ronald LeHew
36-40: Dennis Hockerman
41: Ronald LeHew
42-43: Dennis Hockerman; Ronald LeHew
44: Dennis Hockerman; Ronald LeHew
45: Dennis Hockerman
48-49: Robert Byrd; Bill Morrison

50-51: Christine di Monda
52-53: Heidi Palmer
54-55: Christine di Monda; Heidi Palmer
57: Heidi Palmer
59: Christine di Monda
60-61: Robert Byrd; Christine di Monda
62-63: Robert Byrd
64-65: Heidi Palmer
71: Robert Byrd
74-81: Susan Lexa
84-86: Diane Paterson; George Suyeoka
87: Diane Paterson
88-89: Diane Paterson; George Suyeoka
90-91: Diane Paterson
92: George Suyeoka; Diane Paterson
93-97: George Suyeoka
104-114: Yoshi Miyake
115-121: Kathy Clo
124: Angela Adams
126-127: Diane Paterson
128-129: Susan Lexa
130-133: Christine di Monda

135: Diane Paterson
137: Christine di Monda
140-147: George Suyeoka
148-149: Denise Bohoy; George Suyeoka
152-153: Robert Byrd; Christine di Monda
155: Christine di Monda
156-157: Robert Byrd; Heidi Palmer
158: Heidi Palmer
159: Robert Byrd
161: Bill Morrison
168-169: Susan Lexa; Yoshi Miyake
170-171: Kathy Clo; Yoshi Miyake
172: Susan Lexa
174-175: Susan Lexa
176-177: Yoshi Miyake
194-195: Diane Paterson; Ronald LeHew
196: Diane Paterson
197-199: George Suyeoka
200: Ronald LeHew
201: George Suyeoka

# Preface

Everyone loves a puzzle, whether it's a riddle, a tricky question, a "brain teaser," or a code to be solved. Puzzles are fun. They challenge our imagination and make us think.

But puzzles are more than just a way to have fun. They are also a way of learning **how** to think. It seems that the more puzzles you do, the easier they are to solve. And it seems that as you find it easier to solve puzzles, it is easier for you to solve all kinds of problems!

Puzzles can also help you learn things without even realizing it. One of the world's greatest astronomers once said that he does not think mathematics should be taught in schools. He thinks children could learn it more easily by doing puzzles.

So, here is a book full of puzzles of all kinds. If you are like most people, you will have fun trying to solve them all. And at the same time, you may learn something. Most of all, though, don't be disappointed if you cannot solve a puzzle. Read the answer carefully so you can see how it was worked out. Then you will find that the next puzzle may be a little easier.

# and Seek

In most of these puzzles, you have to look for something that is hidden. It may be a lot of little pictures hidden inside a big one. It may be two things that are just alike, hidden among a lot of things that look different. Or, there may be a lot of things that are all mixed up, and you have to pick out just the right one. But, whatever it is, the best way to find it is by looking very carefully.

# Where's Rover?

The children's dog is lost in the middle of the lumberyard! Can you show them which path they have to take to find him?

(answer on page 28)

# The last acorn

For weeks, Sammy Squirrel and his friend Tammy have been gathering acorns. Now, there is only one acorn left. Can you show Sammy which branch leads to the acorn? And remember, it's not fair to jump from one branch to another!

(answer on page 28)

# Which balloon?

Victoria has just bought a balloon. The monkey is handing her the string. Which balloon is attached to the string?

(answer on page 28)

# Rhyming pairs

On this page there are five pairs of things whose names rhyme. Can you match each pair?

(answers on page 29)

# Ladybugs, ladybugs!

Which two ladybugs look exactly alike?

(answer on page 29)

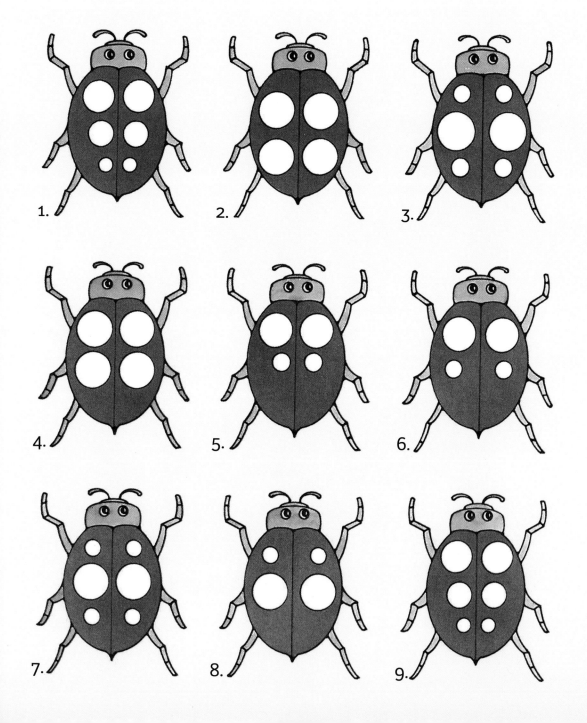

1.

2.

3.

4.

5.

6.

7.

8.

9.

# Ollie the Octopus

Which shadow exactly matches Ollie's picture?

(answer on page 29)

# What's missing?

The pictures on these two pages seem to be just the same. But if you look closely, you'll see they're not. Some of the things in the picture on the left-hand page are missing from the picture on the right-hand page. Can you find what things are missing?

(answer on page 29)

# Mixed-up snakes

One of these five snakes is different from all the others.
Can you find it?

(answer on page 30)

# Lost equipment

A group of children went camping. They lost the eight important things shown at right. The eight things are all hidden somewhere in the picture below. Can you find them?

(answers on page 30)

tent

sleeping bag

coffee pot     first-aid kit     backpack     campfire

flashlight

canoe

# Squares and triangles

Hidden among all the squares and triangles are three
shapes that are *not* squares or triangles. Can you find them?

(answers on page 31)

# Eye foolers

The things on this page are all "eye foolers." You may have to look at them in different ways to find the answers.

(answers on page 31)

1. Find the missing piece of pie.

2. Which alligator's eye is closer to the middle alligator's eye?

3. Which elf is taller?

# Rebus

A rebus is a puzzle in which pictures, letters, and numbers stand for words. In some cases, you must subtract a letter from a word, or from the name of an object, to get the right word. This rebus contains three words that mean a lot to everyone.

(answer on page 31)

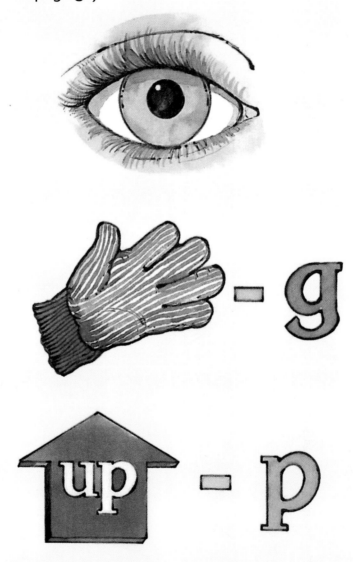

# Picture-words

The first letters in the names of the objects in each row can be put together to make a word. When the three words are put together, they make a sentence. What is the sentence?

(answer on page 31)

# Answers

## Where's Rover? (page 10)

## The last acorn (page 12)

## Which balloon? (page 14)

## Rhyming pairs (page 15)

goat—boat

book—cook

fish—dish

tree—key

mouse—house

## Ladybugs, ladybugs! (page 16)

Numbers 1 and 9 are the same.

## Ollie the Octopus (page 17)

Ollie's shadow is number 5.

## What's missing? (page 18)

The missing things are shown in blue.

## Mixed-up snakes (page 20)

## Lost equipment (page 22)

## Squares and triangles (page 24)

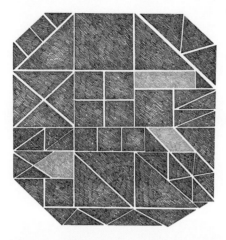

## Eye foolers (page 25)

1. Turn the picture upside down and you'll see the piece of pie.

2. The eyes of both alligators are exactly the same distance from the middle alligator's eye.

3. The elf at the left is taller.

## Rebus (page 26)

I love you

## Picture-words (page 27)

*h*elicopter, *o*wl, *w*indmill:     how

*a*pple, *r*hinoceros, *e*gg:     are

*y*o-yo, *o*strich, *u*mbrella:     you

Riddles are probably the very oldest kind of puzzle. People have been making up riddles and having fun solving them for thousands of years. And some riddles that are thousands of years old are still known to this day.

# Riddles

In olden times, people often used riddles to teach children many of the things they needed to know. Solving riddles is also a way of learning how to solve different kinds of problems. You will find that these riddles will help you get "warmed up" for solving the Brain Teasers and some of the other kinds of puzzles in this book. (NOTE: The answer is right underneath each riddle. You may want to cover the answer until you have had a chance to solve the riddle.)

# Riddles from long ago

Most of these riddles are hundreds of years old. The first one is more than two thousand years old!

What creature walks on four legs in the morning, two legs in the afternoon, and three legs in the evening?

A person. As a baby, in the *morning* of life, a person crawls on all fours. As a grown-up, in the *noontime* of life, a person walks on two legs. As an older man or woman, in the *evening* of life, a person sometimes uses a cane.

Runs all day, but never walks;
Often murmurs, but never talks;
It has a bed, but never sleeps;
It has a mouth, but never eats.

A river.

What flies forever and rests never?

The wind.

The more you feed it,
The more it will grow high.
But if you give it water,
Then it will simply die.
*What is it?*

    Fire.


There may be a houseful or a holeful,
But you cannot catch a bowlful.
*What is it?*

    Smoke.


What kind of water never freezes?

    Hot water.


What grows bigger the more you take from it?

    A hole in the ground.


A box without hinges, a key, or lid,
Yet, golden treasure inside is hid.
*What is it?*

    An egg.


What grows with its roots upward in winter and cannot grow in summer?

    An icicle.

What has teeth but cannot bite?

A comb.

Alive without breath;
As cold as death.
Never thirsty, ever drinking;
All in mail, never clinking.
*What is it?*

A fish.

What has an eye but cannot see?

A needle.

The King of Cumberland
Gave the Queen of Northumberland
A bottomless container
To put flesh and blood in.
What was it?

A ring for her finger.

# Riddles from many lands

These are some of the favorite riddles of children from many different countries. You may be surprised to find that some of these riddles are like the ones that you know.

## Brazil

A crowd of girls dressed in yellow are peeking out of a grocery store.
*What are they?*

A bunch of bananas.

## Canada

It's as green as grass.
It's as black as coal.
Along comes a hungry soul
And puts it into a red hole.
*What is it?*

A blackberry.

### Norway

What is the strongest animal of all?

> The snail. It carries its house around.

### Germany

Why did Hannibal cross the Alps?

> He wanted to get to the other side.

### Italy

Why did General Garibaldi wear red, white, and green suspenders to the Battle of Calatafimi?

> To hold his pants up.

### Africa (Kxatla people)

A white horse goes into the stable and comes out brown. *What is it?*

> A loaf of bread. The dough is white when it goes into the oven (stable) and brown when it comes out, after it is baked.

### Israel

I'm not an airplane, but I fly through the sky. I'm not a river, but I'm full of water. *What am I?*

> A cloud.

### Russia

What kind of a bush does a fox sit under during a rainstorm?

A wet one.

### China

What is it that is made dirty by washing?

Water.

### India

Who never speaks until he is slapped, then cries out in a deep voice?

A drum.

### Egypt

Why does a pelican stand with one leg off the ground?

Because it would fall down if it tried to
stand with both legs off the ground.

### England

It's in rock but not in stone,
It's in marrow but not in bone,
It's in a bolster but not in a bed,
It's not in the live and not in the dead.
*What is it?*

The letter r.

### France

Which is heavier, a pound of feathers or
a pound of lead?

They both weigh the same. A pound is a pound
no matter what it's made of.

### Ireland

A white barn with two roofs and no door at all, at all.
*What is it?*

An egg.

### Japan

What has six legs but walks on only four?

A man on a horse.

## Mexico

Why is a guitar like a comb?

Neither one of them can climb a tree.

## Poland

What does a pig have that even a king doesn't have?

An owner.

## Puerto Rico

I come from San Juan, talking like a priest.
I have a little green body and a red heart on my chest.
*What am I?*

A parrot.

## Scotland

Round and round the rugged rock,
The ragged rascal ran.
How many r's are there in that?
Tell me quickly, if you can.

There are no r's in *that*.

## Sweden

What travels in all directions,
yet is never on the ground or in the air?

A fish.

# Joke riddles

The answers to these riddles really don't make much sense. But they're funny!

GENUINE FUR

Why does a bear have a fur coat?

Because it would look silly in a raincoat.

Name six things that have milk in them.

Ice cream, cocoa, pudding, and three cows.

What has a hundred legs, but can't walk a single step?

Fifty pairs of pants.

**Why did the little boy take a ruler to bed with him?**

Because he wanted to find out how long he was asleep.

**What's the longest word in the dictionary?**

Smile—there's a mile after the first letter.

**Which is faster, heat or cold?**

Heat, because you can catch cold.

**What time is it if a grandfather clock strikes thirteen times?**

Time to get the clock fixed!

**A coffin maker was making a coffin. But every time he tried to hammer a nail into it, it slid away from him. He had to keep chasing it around the workshop! How could he stop the coffin?**

He should give it a cough drop. That usually stops coffin.

**Why were ancient Egyptian boys and girls such good children?**

Because they respected their mummies.

**What bus once crossed an ocean?**

Colum-bus.

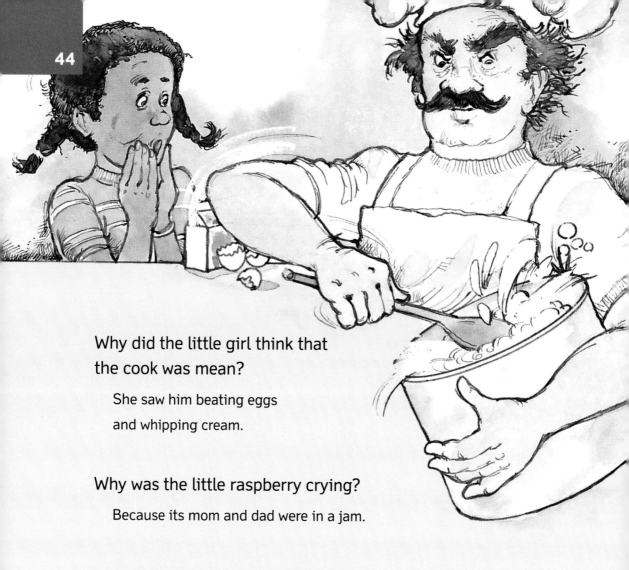

Why did the little girl think that
the cook was mean?

>She saw him beating eggs
>and whipping cream.

Why was the little raspberry crying?

>Because its mom and dad were in a jam.

Why do birds fly south for the winter?

>Because it's too far to walk.

Why isn't it a good idea to go for a walk on an empty stomach?

Because it's easier to walk on a sidewalk.

What does an envelope say when it's licked?

It just shuts up and doesn't say anything.

What animal can jump higher than a mountain?

Any animal. A mountain can't jump!

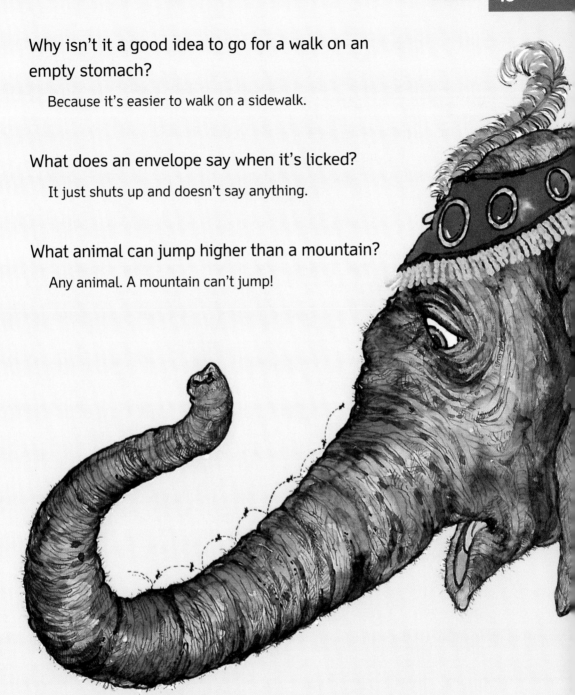

What's the difference between an elephant and a flea?

An elephant can have fleas, but a flea can't have elephants.

Brain

# Teasers

These puzzles are real foolers. They are not quite what they seem to be. They are intended to show you that what may seem to be a difficult problem often has an easy answer. In fact, the answer may be "right under your nose."

So, here is a hint for doing these puzzles. Don't look for a complicated answer. The answer is usually very simple and is hidden in what the puzzle says.

# Three into twelve

There are twelve one-cent stamps in a dozen. How many three-cent stamps are in a dozen?

(answer on page 66)

# Two's from fifty

How many times can you subtract the number two from the number fifty?

(answer on page 66)

# Mr. Chugginmugger's eggs

Every morning, it takes Mr. Finster Chugginmugger three minutes to boil an egg for his breakfast. One day, two friends joined him for breakfast. How long will it take him to boil three eggs?

(answer on page 66)

# The mysterious tunnel

Not far outside the town of Pottsville, a railroad track runs through a tunnel in a hillside. There is only one track, and the tunnel is wide enough for only one train. But one day, two trains went into the tunnel from opposite directions. Each train entered the tunnel at exactly eight o'clock. Three minutes later, each train came out at the opposite end of the tunnel. Yet there was no collision! How was this possible?

(answer on page 66)

# A rainy day mystery

A brother and sister were waiting for the school bus. The morning had been bright and sunny, but now the sky started to cloud over. There was a sprinkle of rain, then a shower, then a cloudburst. The rain lasted for five minutes. The children had no umbrellas or raincoats, and there was no shelter where the bus stopped. But when the bus came, a few minutes after the rain stopped, the two children were perfectly dry. How was this possible?

(answer on page 67)

# The speechless parrot

A man bought a parrot at a pet shop. The owner of the pet shop guaranteed that the parrot could repeat any word it heard. The man took the parrot home, but it never spoke a single word. Nevertheless, what the pet shop owner had said was absolutely true—the parrot *could* repeat any word it heard. So, why didn't it talk?

(answer on page 67)

# The wizard's problem

The old wizard of Wallapoo lived alone in a tall tower on a hilltop. One day, he decided to take a bath.

The bathroom was at the very top of the tower. It was a small room, with only one door and no windows. The walls, floor, and ceiling were made of stone.

The wizard got into the tub and turned on the water. Just then, his cat chased a mouse past the door. The cat bumped into the door and it swung shut with a thump. The bump jarred the latch, and the wizard heard it click. He was locked in the bathroom!

Angrily, the wizard turned off the faucet—and the handle broke off in his hand. Water continued to pour out of the faucet. There was no way to shut it off. Slowly, the water began to fill the bathtub. The wizard knew that in time the whole room would be filled with water—and he couldn't get out!

How did the wizard keep from drowning?

(He *didn't* use magic.)

(answer on page 67)

# The nut collectors

Six squirrels began to gather hickory nuts and put them into a large basket. The squirrels worked so fast that the number of nuts in the basket was doubled at the end of every minute. The basket was completely full at the end of ten minutes. How many minutes had it taken the squirrels to get the basket half full?

(answer on page 67)

# A sailor's puzzle

Long ago, a ship was anchored in the port of Amsterdam. A rope ladder hung over the ship's side. There were sixteen rungs in the ladder. The bottom rung of the ladder just touched the water.

Every half hour, the tide rose exactly one-half the distance between two rungs of the ladder. How long did it take for the water to cover four rungs of the ladder?

(answer on page 68)

# The prisoner

Pietro, the brave young leader of the rebels, had been captured by the soldiers of the wicked Duke Malvolio. They took him to the castle and put him into the dungeon.

"Tomorrow morning, the Duke will have you hanged," said the captain of the soldiers. Then, grinning wickedly, he slammed the heavy wooden door and locked it.

Young Pietro looked around the empty cell. It was square, with walls and ceiling made of stone. The floor was bare earth. On one wall there was a narrow window. Pietro thought he could squeeze through the window if he could reach it. But it was so high up that he couldn't reach it even by jumping.

Pietro was in despair. Tomorrow he was to die, and there seemed no way to escape!

Suddenly, he threw himself down on the floor and began to dig in the dirt with his hands. He had thought of a way to escape through the window by digging a hole in the floor! Do you know what he planned to do?

(answer on page 68)

# The amazing rabbit

Two rabbits were nibbling clover in a meadow. They were facing in opposite directions. Suddenly, one cried out to the other: "Look out! There's a fox sneaking up behind you!"

The rabbit didn't hear or smell the fox. How did it know the fox was sneaking up behind its friend?

(answer on page 68)

# How did he know?

A man was waiting at an airport for a plane to arrive. Suddenly, he heard someone call his name. Looking up, he saw an old friend of his hurrying toward him.

"Hey, Bill!" called his friend. "How are you? I haven't seen you in years!"

"How are you?" exclaimed Bill. "Wow, you look great!"

"I'm married now, to somebody you don't know," said the other. "This is my daughter."

Bill smiled down at the little girl. "Hi, young lady. What's your name?"

"It's the same as my mama's," said the girl. "Is that so," said Bill, winking at his friend. "Then your name must be Cindy!"

How could he possibly know this?

(answer on page 68)

# The museum

Professor Priscilla Pippen was a history teacher at a college.
One Saturday as she drove through a very small town, she saw
a tiny building with a sign on it. The sign read, "Museum of
Natural History." Professor Pippen parked her car and went
into the museum.

There were only five exhibits in the museum. These were:

1. A prehistoric arrowhead made of copper.

2. The fossil skeleton of a dinosaur no bigger than a chicken.

3. An ancient Roman coin marked with the date 120 B.C.

4. A red diamond in a ring.

5. An ancient Egyptian cat mummy.

Professor Pippen knew at once that one of the exhibits was a
fake. Which one was it?

(answer on page 69)

# Hungry horses

If five horses can eat five bags of oats in five minutes, how long will it take a hundred horses to eat a hundred bags of oats?

(answer on page 69)

# Leftover sandwiches

Mrs. Martin made twenty-four sandwiches for a picnic. All but seven were eaten. How many were left?

(answer on page 69)

# Even money

Two mothers and two daughters decided to go shopping. They found that they had twenty-seven dollars, all in one-dollar bills. They divided up the money evenly, without making any of the dollars into change, so that they each had exactly the same amount. How was this possible?

(answer on page 69)

# A windy day puzzle

It was a windy day in autumn. Most of the leaves had been blown off the trees. The Johnsons' lawn was covered with red, yellow, and brown leaves.

Randy Johnson came out to rake the leaves for his parents. Just for fun, he first raked the leaves into small piles. He made six piles in one corner of the lawn, and half as many piles in another corner. In a third corner there were twice as many piles, and in the fourth corner only a third as many piles.

Randy then began to rake all the leaves into one pile in the middle of the lawn. Just then a gust of wind blew into one of the piles. It picked up all the leaves in the pile and scattered them over the neighborhood! How many piles did Randy finally end up with?

(answer on page 70)

## The tennis player

Once there was a player

In a tennis game.

She played very well,

And won great fame.

Jane was her first name,

What was her last name.

The tennis player's last name is hidden
in the poem. Can you find it?

(answer on page 70)

# Cutting problems

1. You have five pieces of chain. There are three links in each piece.

To fasten two pieces together, you would have to cut a link apart, join it to another link, then close it up.

How many links would you have to cut apart in order to join all five pieces to make one chain?

2. You have a long stick of wood that you want to cut into ten pieces, all the same length. It takes one minute to make each cut. How many minutes will it take to cut the stick into the ten pieces?

(answers on page 71)

# The hungry Vikings

Long ago, a band of Vikings, with their wives and children, made ready for a long journey. They would sail from Norway to Iceland, to make new homes.

They would be at sea for weeks, living on hard crackers and dried, cold meat. They couldn't cook aboard ship for fear of fire. They all knew they would be yearning for a good meal of roast pork when they finally reached land. But any pork they took along would spoil long before they got to Iceland.

Rolf Hairybeard, the Viking chieftain, talked over the problem with some of his men.

"We could tie long ropes to big pieces of meat and let them trail in the water," suggested one man. "That might keep them cool enough so they would not spoil."

"Sharks would eat the meat," Hairybeard pointed out.

"Let's keep the meat aboard ship, but pile up snow and ice around it to keep it cold," said another of the Vikings.

"The ship would get full of water when the ice and snow melted," objected Hairybeard.

"I can tell you how to keep meat fresh for as long as you want," said Hairybeard's wife, Gunnhilda. When she told the men her idea, they all agreed it would work. What was her idea?

(answer on page 71)

## Three into twelve

(page 48)

There are twelve three-cent stamps in a dozen, just as there are twelve one-cent stamps in a dozen. A dozen is twelve of anything.

## Two's from fifty

(page 48)

You can subtract two from fifty only *once*. After that, the fifty is forty-eight.

## Mr. Chugginmugger's eggs

(page 49)

If Mr. Chugginmugger has two guests for breakfast, he will boil their eggs at the same time he boils his own. If one egg will boil in three minutes, then three eggs in the same pot will also boil in three minutes.

## The mysterious tunnel

(page 50)

One train went through the tunnel at eight o'clock in the morning. The other train went through at eight o'clock at night.

## A rainy day mystery

(page 51)

The children were inside their house while they waited for the bus.

## The speechless parrot

(page 51)

The parrot couldn't hear any words to repeat. It was deaf.

## The wizard's problem

(page 52)

To keep from drowning, all the wizard had to do was pull out the plug in the bathtub! But then he had to figure out how to open the door. And that was a lot harder!

## The nut collectors

(page 54)

If the number of nuts in the basket doubled at the end of every minute, the basket must have been half full in nine minutes. Then, after one more minute, the half would be doubled, thus filling the other half of the basket.

## A sailor's puzzle

(page 55)

The water never covered any of the rungs. A ship, of course, floats on water. So, as the tide rose, the ship rose with it. And the rope ladder, which was attached to the ship, also rose.

## The prisoner

(page 56)

By digging a deep hole in the floor of the cell, Pietro could make a large pile of dirt. Then, by standing on the pile of dirt, he could reach the window.

## The amazing rabbit

(page 58)

Although the rabbits were facing in opposite directions, they were facing each other. Thus, the rabbit could *see* the fox sneaking toward his friend.

## How did he know?

(page 58)

Bill knew the little girl's name because it was the same as his friend's name. His old friend, to whom he was talking, was named Cindy, and she was the little girl's mother.

## The museum

(page 59)

The fake exhibit was number 3—the ancient Roman coin marked 120 B.C. The abbreviation B.C. stands for "Before Christ." People who lived 120 years before Christ couldn't possibly have known it, of course! So they would not have put B.C. on any of their coins.

## Hungry horses

(page 60)

If five horses can eat five bags of oats in five minutes, then it takes *each* horse five minutes to eat a bag of oats. Therefore, it will take only five minutes for a hundred horses to eat a hundred bags of oats.

## Leftover sandwiches

(page 60)

If all but seven sandwiches were eaten, then seven sandwiches were left, of course.

## Even money

(page 60)

The two mothers and two daughters were actually only three people—Sue, her mother, and her grandmother. Sue was her mother's daughter, of course, and her mother was the grandmother's daughter—that's two daughters. Sue's mother was one mother, and *her* mother, the grandmother, was the other mother. Thus, they divided the twenty-seven dollars three ways, each taking nine dollars.

## A windy day puzzle

(page 61)

After the gust of wind blew away one of the piles, Randy continued to rake the leaves into one pile in the middle of the lawn. So, of course, he *ended up* with only one pile.

## The tennis player

(page 62)

The tennis player's first *and* last names are given in the last two lines of the poem.

Jane was her first name,

What was her last name.

The two lines make one complete sentence. And there is a period at the end of the sentence, *not* a question mark. So the sentence *tells* something, it doesn't ask a question. It tells you that *Jane* was the player's first name and that *What* was her last name. Her name was Jane What.

## Cutting problems

(page 63)

1. To join all five pieces of chain to make one single chain, you have to cut only the *three* links of one piece. With those three links you can link the other pieces together, as shown.

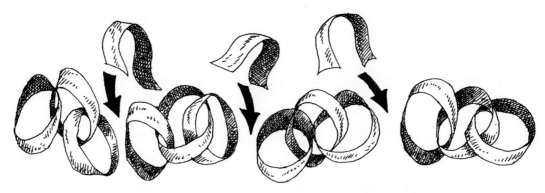

2. It will take you *nine* minutes to cut the stick into ten pieces, because you need to make only nine cuts. The ninth cut turns the last section of wood into two pieces—the ninth and tenth pieces.

## The hungry Vikings

(page 64)

Gunnhilda's idea was to keep some live pigs in a cage on the ship. When the Vikings got to Iceland, they could butcher the animals and have fresh meat for a feast.

# Mystery!

A mystery story is a kind of puzzle. Many people think it is the very best kind of puzzle. They enjoy trying to find the clues and then put them together to solve the crime.

So, if you are the kind of person who likes to play detective, here is a short mystery story. It takes place at night, in a big, old house, during a thunderstorm. The story is filled with clues. If you **spot** them, you can figure out who committed the crime.

# The Mystery of the Chinese Vase

It was one minute after eleven o'clock at night. A torrent of rain poured down out of a pitch-black sky. It drummed on the roof of the big, old house that sat in the middle of a huge yard surrounded by a high iron fence. Two lights burned in rooms on the second floor. Several others glowed on the first floor.

Suddenly, the sky was shattered by a titanic crash of thunder. An instant later, a woman screamed, "Mr. Potney! Mr. Potney!"

On the second floor of the house, a door opened. A young man in pajamas, his hair all mussed and his eyes blinking sleepily, peered out. At the far end of the long hall, a light shone through the doorway of another room. A young woman stood there. When she saw the young man, she came running toward him.

"Jack! Jack!" she cried.

"Elaine, what's the matter?" he asked. "I was asleep, but I thought I heard someone call out. What's happened?"

"Oh, Jack, your uncle has been robbed," Elaine exclaimed. "His Chinese vase has been stolen!"

Just then, a door opened in the middle of the hall. An elderly man, clad in bathrobe and slippers, stepped out.

"Did someone call me?" he asked. "I was taking a shower and couldn't hear well."

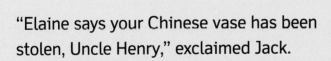

"Elaine says your Chinese vase has been stolen, Uncle Henry," exclaimed Jack.

"Yes, Mr. Potney," the young woman sobbed.

"Good heavens!" gasped Mr. Potney. He ran up the hall toward his bedroom. Jack and Elaine hurried after him.

Against one bedroom wall stood a large wood-en cabinet in which Mr. Potney kept his Chinese vase. The vase was hundreds of years old—and worth thousands of dollars.

The cabinet was always closed and locked. But now, the cabinet door was wide open and the vase was gone!

"Someone pried the door open!" Mr. Potney exclaimed. He looked at the young woman. "How did you find out about this, Elaine?"

"I was downstairs watching television until just a few minutes ago," said Elaine. "When I came upstairs, the door to your room was open. I knew you were taking a shower, so I wondered why the light was on. I looked in and saw the open cabinet. The vase was gone. That's when I called you."

Jack looked at Elaine rather suspiciously. She was his uncle's private secretary, and Jack liked her. But he wondered if she were telling the truth. She could have taken the vase!

Jack's feet were bare, and he suddenly realized that the rug felt damp. Could rain have blown into the room? Maybe the thief had come in through a window and left it open.

Jack looked about. No, all the windows were closed. Then a gleam caught his eye. Lying in a corner of the room was a small kitchen knife. He pointed to it. "Look! I'll bet that's what was used to pry open the cabinet."

Mr. Potney started to pick up the knife, but Jack stopped him. "There may be fingerprints on it, Uncle Henry. We should call the police."

He hurried out of the room and headed for the stairs, the others after him. The stairs were carpeted, and several times Jack thought he felt dampness on his bare feet.

As Jack and the others reached the foot of the stairs, three people came hurrying toward them. One was chubby Mrs. Elson, the cook. Behind her were tall, thin Julian, the chauffeur, and sturdy Mr. Stokes, the butler. Mrs. Elson and Julian were fully dressed. Stokes was in pajamas, bathrobe, and slippers. But, of course, his gray hair was neatly combed. Stokes always managed to look well-groomed.

"We heard someone call out," panted Mrs. Elson. "Is there a fire?"

Jack stared at her for a moment. He knew that the knife that had been used to pry open the cabinet was one of the knives she used in the kitchen. Could she be the thief? "My uncle's priceless Chinese vase has been stolen," he told her.

Mrs. Elson gasped, and looked as if she were going to faint. While the others fussed over her, Jack walked into the next room. This was the room in which Elaine said she had been watching television. He put his hand on the television set. It was still warm. The set had certainly been on until only a short time ago, but that didn't prove that Elaine had been there all the time.

Jack thought about what she had said. She, and everyone else, knew that Mr. Potney always took a shower at about a quarter to eleven each night. Jack looked at the clock on the

wall. The time was now five minutes after eleven. It was only a minute or so after eleven when Elaine's cry had awakened him. So, whoever had stolen the vase must have done so between a quarter to eleven and eleven o'clock.

There was a mirror on the wall by the clock. Jack caught sight of his mussed hair, sticking out in all directions from when he had been asleep. He tried combing it with his fingers. Then he went back into the other room.

"Elaine," he said, "did you see anyone go upstairs while you were watching television?"

"No," she replied. "You can't see the stairs from where I was sitting."

"Did you see or hear anything at all?"

"Well, at about a quarter to eleven, Mrs. Elson looked in and said goodnight," the girl told him.

"That's right," said Mrs. Elson, nodding her head. "I had just left the kitchen and was going to my room."

"Did you go straight to your room?"

"Oh, yes," the women assured him.

"That's true, sir," said Stokes, the butler. "I saw Mrs. Elson as she left the kitchen, and she saw me. I was just bringing the dog in from its walk. It started to rain while I was outside, and as Mrs. Elson can tell you, I was soaking wet. I went right to my room, took off my wet clothes, and went to bed."

"Your room is right under my uncle's," said Jack, thoughtfully. "Did you hear anyone walking around up there?"

"No," said Stokes. "I was already asleep when Julian and Mrs. Elson pounded at my door and said they'd heard shouts. I thought there was a fire, so I just threw on my robe and slippers and rushed out."

Jack looked at the chauffeur. "What about you, Julian? Where were you from about a quarter to eleven to eleven o'clock?"

Julian wriggled nervously. "I said goodnight to Stokes about ten-thirty. I was in my room reading, until I heard Elaine call out."

"I see," said Jack, slowly. He had a good idea who the thief was!

Do *you* know who it was?

# How Jack solved the crime

Several things that Stokes said convinced Jack that the butler was the thief.

When Stokes mentioned getting soaking wet in the rain, Jack realized that the damp spots on the rug in his uncle's room and on the stairs could have been caused by the butler's wet shoes and dripping clothing.

Jack also realized that Stokes would have known that no one would see him if he went upstairs. Stokes knew that Julian was in his room because they had said goodnight to one another at ten-thirty. The butler also knew that Mrs. Elson would be out of the way, for he had seen her leaving for her room when he brought the dog in. And he also knew that Elaine couldn't see the stairs from where she was sitting.

So, when Stokes brought the dog in, he saw his chance. But he would have to hurry before the news show that Elaine was watching ended. He took a knife from the kitchen, hurried upstairs, and stole the vase. Then he went to his room, got out of his wet clothes and put on his pajamas. But instead of going to bed, he waited to see what would happen.

But, because he was a neat person, Stokes combed his hair. This, too, was a clue for Jack. For when Jack looked into the mirror, he saw that his hair was mussed from sleeping. Stokes had said that he had been asleep, but his hair was neatly combed. Jack knew that if Stokes had been asleep, his hair, too, would have been mussed.

One meaning of the word "shuffle" is "to move something around, this way and that." And this is what you do to solve these puzzles. The puzzles show you how to make shapes and designs out of toothpicks, coins, or buttons. Then you have to change the shapes to something else. To make the change, you just shuffle, or move, the objects around until you have the right shape.

# Shufflers

Sounds easy? Don't be too sure! Sometimes it will seem that you simply can't change the shape the way the puzzle wants you to! But keep trying—it can be done. And, be sure to read each puzzle carefully, for sometimes there is a clue hidden in what the puzzle says.

# The spilled ice cream

Arrange two toothpicks and a large coin or button like this:

Think of this shape as an ice-cream cone with one scoop of ice cream in it. Can you move one toothpick so that the ice-cream cone is upside down and the ice cream (the coin) is no longer inside the cone?

(answer on page 98)

# House into squares

Using six toothpicks, make a "house" like this:

Now, moving only two toothpicks, change the "house" into five squares.

(answer on page 98)

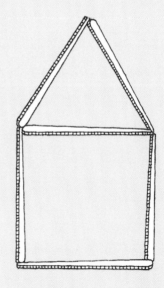

# Save the sea horse!

Using nine toothpicks, make a "fish" like the one shown here:

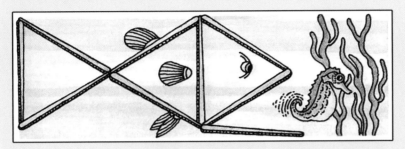

This fish is hungry! As you can see, its mouth is open and it is about to swallow a baby sea horse! Can you save the sea horse by changing the fish into four triangles, as shown below? But to do this, you may move only *three* toothpicks!

(answer on page 98)

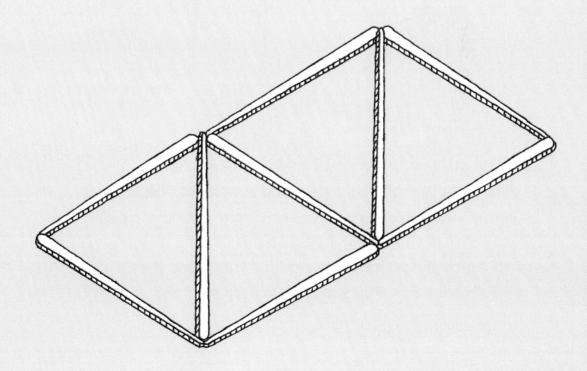

# The Smiths and Kents

With eighteen toothpicks, make two "houses" and a "yard" as shown below. Place four buttons, as shown, for "trees."

The house on the left belongs to the Smith family. The house on the right belongs to the Kent family. Each family owns half the yard. But they can't figure out how to divide it so that each family will have two trees. Using no more than three toothpicks, build a fence that will divide the yard into two equal parts, with two trees in each part.

(answer on page 98)

# Ice-cream sundae

Arrange four toothpicks and a small button or coin this way:

This is an ice-cream sundae glass with a cherry in it! Can you turn the glass upside down and get the cherry out by moving only two toothpicks?

(answer on page 98)

# Too many monkeys

1. For this puzzle you will need nine toothpicks and four small buttons or coins. Arrange the toothpicks to make three triangles. Put a button inside each triangle. One button is left over.

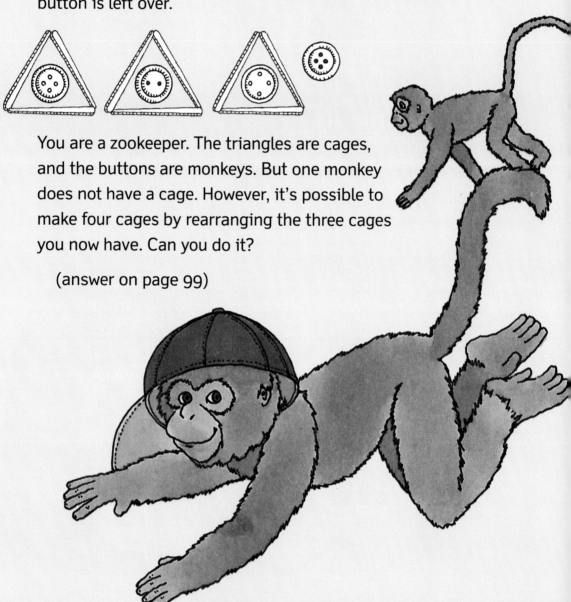

You are a zookeeper. The triangles are cages, and the buttons are monkeys. But one monkey does not have a cage. However, it's possible to make four cages by rearranging the three cages you now have. Can you do it?

(answer on page 99)

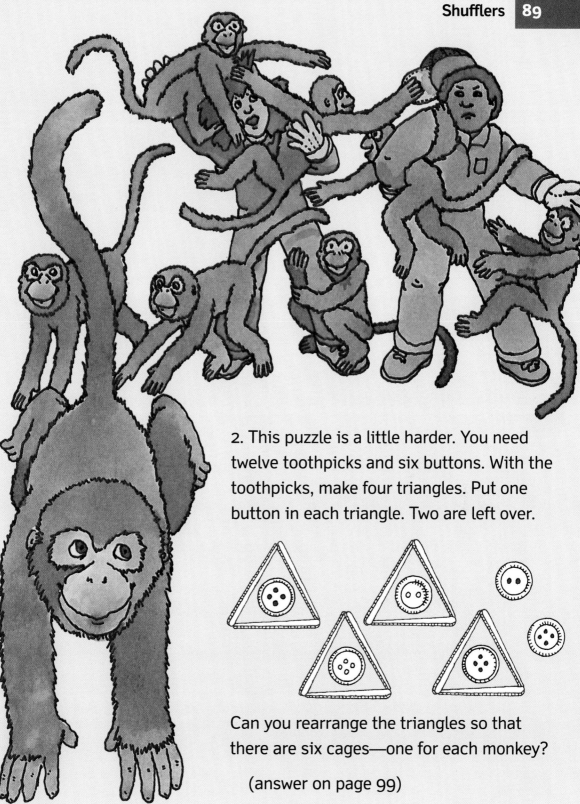

2. This puzzle is a little harder. You need twelve toothpicks and six buttons. With the toothpicks, make four triangles. Put one button in each triangle. Two are left over.

Can you rearrange the triangles so that there are six cages—one for each monkey?

(answer on page 99)

# Triangle turnaround

Using buttons or coins, set up a triangle like the one shown here. Then, by moving only *three* of the buttons, see if you can turn the whole triangle around to face the other way, with the point at the bottom!

(answer on page 99)

# Three in a row

1. Lay three pennies or other coins in a row. The middle coin should be tails up. The other coins should be heads up. Turning over only one coin at a time, make all three coins heads up in three moves.

2. Lay three coins in a row, as before, with the middle one tails up and the other two heads up. Turning over two coins at a time, make all the coins tails up in three moves.

3. Lay three coins in a row. Change the position of the middle coin—that is, get it out of the middle—without touching it!

(answers on page 99)

# The farmer

Arrange eight toothpicks like this:

1. A prosperous farmer had a piece of land that was this shape. He wanted to divide the land into six equal parts, because he planned to grow a different crop in each part. Using five more toothpicks, can you divide the land into six equal parts?

2. One day, the farmer decided that he ought to have a will. So, he went to see his lawyer. The farmer told the lawyer that when he died, he wanted to leave one-third of his land to his wife. He wanted another third divided into two equal parts for his two sons. And he wanted to divide the last third into four equal parts for his four grandchildren.

Using the five toothpicks you used to divide the farmer's land into six parts, can you show the lawyer how to divide the land the way the farmer wants to do it?

(answers on page 100)

# Can it be done?

1. It's easy to arrange fifteen buttons in five rows with three buttons in each row.

But can you arrange *seven* buttons in five rows with three buttons in each row?

2. It's easy to arrange twenty buttons in five rows with four buttons in each row. But can you arrange *ten* buttons in five rows with four buttons in each row?

(answers on page 100)

# The mouse king's treasure

The king of the mice had a treasury. It was a big room, full of all kinds of cheese! He kept the room locked, of course. And he kept the key on a tiny island surrounded by a deep, eight-sided moat. In the moat swam deadly sharp-toothed sharks.

When the king wanted some cheese, he had his mouseke-teer guards carry a small boat down to the moat. He rowed out to the island, got the key, and rowed back. When the boat wasn't in use, it was kept locked away.

The king felt sure that none of his subjects could ever get the key to the cheese treasury. But, one night, a rascally mouse by the name of Cheeky managed to steal the key! He did this using only two toothpicks.

On the opposite page, there is a picture of the moat and island. It is the same size as the king's moat and island. Using two toothpicks, see if you can figure out how Cheeky got across the moat. But remember, the toothpicks must not touch the water.

(answer on page 101)

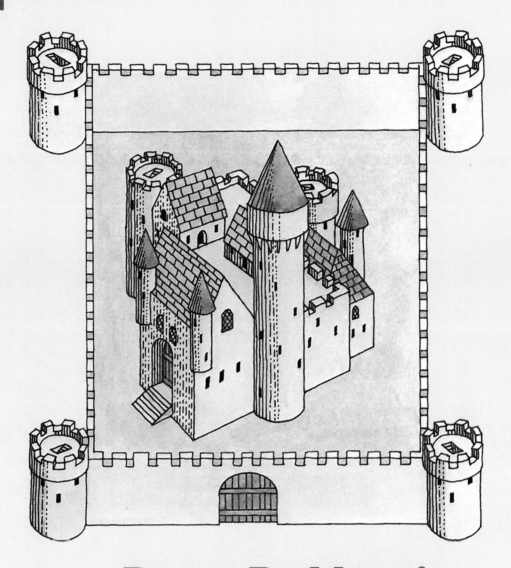

# Baron Baddguy's wall

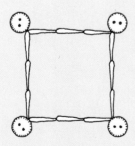

The castle of Baron Baddguy is surrounded by a square wall. At each corner of the wall there is a round tower. To make a plan of the wall and towers, arrange twelve toothpicks and four buttons, as shown at left.

Baron Baddguy wants to double the space inside the wall. But he wants the wall to be square and he wants to keep the four towers just where they are, on the outside of the wall. Can you show him how to do this?

You can use the twelve toothpicks, plus four more. You may move the toothpicks any way you wish. But the new wall must form a square and it must enclose twice as much space as the old wall. The four towers can not be moved, and they must be outside the new wall.

(answer on page 101)

# Answers

## The spilled ice cream (page 84)

To turn the cone upside down, simply move one of the toothpicks to the right (or left), as shown.

## House into squares (page 84)

Move the two toothpicks that form the roof so as to make a cross inside the square, as shown. This makes four small squares inside one large square, or a total of five squares.

## Save the sea horse! (page 85)

The toothpicks to be moved are shown in blue.

## The Smiths and Kents (page 86)

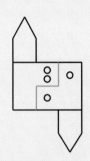

## Ice-cream sundae (page 87)

To turn the glass upside down, first slide the horizontal toothpick over, as shown in (B) below. Then move the leftover toothpick to form the other side of the glass, as shown in (C).

A          B          C

## Too many monkeys (pages 88-89) 1  2

## Triangle turnaround (page 90)

Move the end buttons on the bottom row to the second row. Move the button that's on top to the bottom.

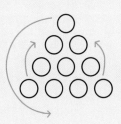

## Three in a row (page 91)

1.　　Ⓗ　Ⓣ　Ⓗ

(a) Turn over the coin on the right.　　Ⓗ　Ⓣ　Ⓣ

(b) Turn over the coin in the middle.　　Ⓗ　Ⓗ　Ⓣ

(c) Turn over the coin on the right.　　Ⓗ　Ⓗ　Ⓗ

2.　　Ⓗ　Ⓣ　Ⓗ

(a) Turn over the coins on the ends.　　Ⓣ　Ⓣ　Ⓣ

(b) Turn over the coin in the middle
　　and the coin on the right.　　Ⓣ　Ⓗ　Ⓗ

(c) Turn over the coin in the middle
　　and the coin on the right.　　Ⓣ　Ⓣ　Ⓣ

3.

Move the coin on the left (or right) so that the middle coin becomes an outside coin without being touched.

## The farmer (page 92)

1. The five toothpicks that divide the shape into six parts are shown in blue.

2. To divide the shape into thirds, place two toothpicks as shown in (A) at left.

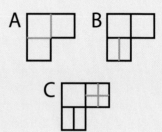

Leave one-third for the farmer's wife. Using one toothpick, divide another third in half for the farmer's sons, as shown in (B).

Divide the last third into four equal parts by placing one toothpick across another as shown in (C).

## Can it be done? (page 93)

1. Arrange the seven buttons as shown at right. This gives you five rows of three buttons, as shown by the blue lines.

2. Arrange the ten buttons as shown. This gives you five rows of four buttons, as shown by the blue lines.

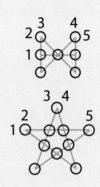

## The mouse king's treasure (page 94)

First, Cheeky placed one toothpick across an angle of the pond so that its ends rested on the ground. Then he placed the second toothpick with one end resting on the first toothpick and the other end resting on the island, as shown. Thus, he was able to scamper across the second toothpick, get the key, and scamper back.

## Baron Baddguy's wall (page 96)

The new wall, made of 16 toothpicks, is shown in black. The old wall is shown in blue. The new wall encloses exactly twice as much space as the old wall. The towers haven't been moved and are still outside the wall.

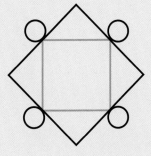

The word *ponder* means "to think over carefully." And that is what it takes to solve these puzzles.

In some of the puzzles you have to move things from one place to another, in a certain way. There really aren't any clues in this kind of puzzle. It might help if you used coins or other objects to represent the things being moved. Then you could try moving them in different ways.

In other puzzles you have to decide what kind of question someone might ask to get a certain

# Ponderers

answer. There aren't any clues for this kind of puzzle, either. You have to ask yourself questions and see what the answers might be. Sooner or later, you will get an idea of what the right sort of question is.

And one or two of the puzzles are really just based on common sense. You have to ask yourself, "How would *I* do this?"

Don't give up too easily. When you solve one of these puzzles, you really can be proud.

# How many carnations?

Wilfred McDoodle was color blind. Red and green both looked the same color to him.

Wilfred got a job working for a florist. One day, when he was all alone in the store, a lady came in and wanted to buy either two red or two green carnations. She didn't care which color they were so long as they were both the same.

Wilfred knew there were a dozen red carnations and a dozen green carnations all mixed together in the refrigerator in the back room of the store. But the red and green carnations all looked the same to him. Would he have to bring all two dozen carnations so the lady could pick out two of the same color?

What is the smallest number of carnations Wilfred would have to bring back to be sure of having two of the same color?

(answer on page 118)

# Sooba the cider seller

Cider is the national drink of the land of Bulgravia. On the main street of every town there is at least one cider shop. The cider is kept in big barrels. It's sold in amounts known as "guzzles." (A guzzle is about equal to one cup or 250 milliliters, but that isn't important.)

One day, a customer came into the cider shop of a lady named Sooba. The customer had a large bucket. He asked Sooba to put exactly four guzzles of cider into the bucket.

Sooba took the bucket to the cider barrel. Next to the barrel there was a three-guzzle pitcher and a five-guzzle pitcher. How could Sooba measure out exactly four guzzles of cider?

(answer on page 118)

# The people of Tuffleheim

Long ago, a traveler walking along a road met a man coming the other way. "Hello, friend," called the man. "Where are you heading?"

"I am going to the town of Tuffleheim," said the traveler.

"Oh, you will need to be careful, there," warned the other man. "That town has been enchanted by a wicked magician! Half the people can tell only the truth, and the other half can tell only lies. You never know whom to believe in Tuffleheim."

"I will be careful," said the traveler.

An hour later, he reached Tuffleheim. It was getting late, and he was tired and hungry. He wanted to find a good inn where he could have a nice dinner and a comfortable room in which to spend the night. In any other town, he would have simply asked someone for the name of the best inn. But he couldn't do that, here. For, if the person he asked should happen to be one of the liars, he would send the traveler to the *worst* inn.

The traveler realized he would have to first find out whether anyone he talked to was a liar or a truth-teller. He went up to the first Tuffleheimer he saw and asked her a question. What question could the traveler have asked that would let him know, at once, whether a person was a liar or a truth-teller?

(answer on page 118)

# The outlaws and the marshals

Sheriff Dalton of Dry Gulch heard that two U.S. marshals were searching for some outlaws near his town. He decided to ride out and see if he could help them.

After a time, he saw a campfire with four men around it. Riding closer, he saw that two of the men were tied up and two were untied.

"Are you the marshals?" he called to the untied men.

One of the men said something, but Sheriff Dalton could not hear him. "What did you say?" he called.

The second man answered. "He said that we're the marshals."

Suddenly, one of the tied-up men began to struggle. "That is not true!" he yelled.

"*We're* the marshals! We set out to capture these two, but they ambushed us! They are the outlaws!"

Sheriff Dalton knew that the marshals would always tell the truth. He also knew that the outlaws would always tell lies. How could he know from what the men said, which ones were really the marshals and which ones were the outlaws?

(answer on page 119)

# Caspuccio the bandit

In the Kingdom of Cappedonia, there was a daring bandit named Caspuccio. But he robbed only barons, earls, and wealthy nobles. And he gave much of the money he stole to poor people who needed it. So, most common people liked him. Of course, the barons and earls hated him.

Finally, Caspuccio was captured. He was taken before King Bombaso, for trial. All the barons and earls came to the trial. So did many common people.

"So, this is the famous robber, Caspuccio," said the king. "What shall we do with him?"

"Hang him!" yelled all the barons.

"Cut off his head!" shouted the earls.

"Set him free!" cried the common people.

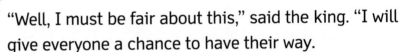

"Well, I must be fair about this," said the king. "I will give everyone a chance to have their way. Caspuccio, I want you to make a statement. In other words, *tell* me something. If what you say is true, you will be hanged, as the barons want. If what you say is false, you will have your head cut off, as the earls want. But if I can not decide if it is true or false, you will go free, as the common people want."

Caspuccio knew he did not have much of a chance. After all, every statement is either true or false! The king could say that what Caspuccio said was either true or false.

Caspuccio thought for a few moments. Then, a smile came over his face. He spoke seven words. And after thinking about what he said for a while, the king set him free!

What did Caspuccio say?

(answer on page 119)

# The three musicians

Long ago, in China, three musicians were traveling to the city of Beijing. They had been hired to perform at a wedding there.

The three came to a wide river. They were shocked to see that the bridge had collapsed. There was no way to get across the river. The musicians knew that the nearest bridge was far down the river, nearly a day's walk away. But they had to be in Beijing in a few hours.

Suddenly, they saw two children rowing a boat down the river. The musicians called to the children, offering to pay them to use the boat. The children rowed to the shore.

However, the boat was *very* small. It could hold only two children or one grown-up. This was a serious problem. If one of the musicians took the boat across the river, there would be no way to send the boat back. A grown-up could not take a child and then send the child back with the boat—for a grown-up and child could not both get into the boat at the same time.

But one of the children had an idea.
And in less than an hour, all three
musicians were across the river.
How did they do it?

(answer on page 120)

# Abdul's journeys

An Arab named Abdul made a journey from his home to another part of the desert.

For the first half of the journey, Abdul got to ride in a truck. It was a one-hour ride. And going by truck was ten times faster than Abdul could have walked the same distance.

However, for the second half of the journey, Abdul had to ride an old, lame camel. That part of the trip took him twice as long as if he had walked.

When Abdul went back home, he had to walk all the way. Which of the two trips was quickest? How much time did each trip take?

(answer on page 120)

# The bad bears

One day, Mrs. Bear went to market and left her four little cubs, Bruno, Boffin, Bobo, and Bilda, alone in the house. Of course, the four got into mischief! When Mrs. Bear returned, she found a broken honeypot and a big puddle of honey on the living room floor!

"Who broke the honeypot?" demanded Mrs. Bear.

"I didn't do it," cried Bruno.

"Bobo did it," claimed Boffin.

"Bilda did it," said Bobo.

"Bobo's lying!" exclaimed Bilda.

Three of the little bears are lying. One is telling the truth. Who is telling the truth? And which bear broke the honeypot?

(answer on page 121)

# The Ping-Pong and the Biggie

Explorers from Earth landed on a far-off planet. They were amazed to find that all the creatures on the planet were shaped like balls! These creatures could not bounce, but they could move by rolling.

The smartest creatures were about the size of a ping-pong ball. The Earth people called them "Ping-Pongs." There was another kind of creature that was ten times bigger than a Ping-Pong. The Earth people called these things "Biggies." They noticed that anytime a Biggie saw a Ping-Pong, the Biggie would try to roll over the little Ping-Pong and crush it!

The Earth people built a small, one-room hut to live in while they were on the planet. When they left the planet, they left this hut empty, with the door open.

One day, a Ping-Pong came rolling into the hut. It was amazed by the square room with the four sharp corners. Ping-Pongs had never imagined such a thing.

Suddenly, a Biggie came rolling into the hut. It was between the Ping-Pong and the door—the only way out. The Ping-Pong was trapped! The Biggie rolled toward it!

But the Ping-Pong was clever. It found a way to keep the Biggie from rolling over it. What did the Ping-Pong do?

(answer on page 121)

## How many carnations? (page 104)

The smallest number of carnations Wilfred McDoodle would have to bring back would be *three*. When he picked out two carnations, they might both be the same color, but one might be red and one might be green. Therefore, by taking along a third flower that would be either red or green he would be sure of having two carnations of the same color.

## Sooba the cider seller (page 105)

Sooba filled the three-guzzle pitcher and poured the three guzzles into the bucket. Then she filled the three-guzzle pitcher again and poured the three guzzles into the five-guzzle pitcher. She filled the three-guzzle pitcher a third time. She then poured the cider into the five-guzzle pitcher until it was filled. It took two guzzles to fill the five-guzzle pitcher (with the three already in it), which left exactly one guzzle in the three-guzzle pitcher. Sooba poured the one guzzle into the bucket, which already had three guzzles in it. She now had four guzzles in the bucket.

## The people of Tuffleheim (page 106)

The traveler must ask a question to which he knows the answer. Then he will know whether the answer he got was true or false. He could ask a question with an obvious answer, such as "Is it daytime?" or "Am I a man?" A truth-teller would, of course, give the right answer, but a liar would reveal himself by giving an answer the traveler knows is wrong.

## The outlaws and the marshals
(page 108)

The sheriff knew that if the man who answered first had been an outlaw, he would have lied and said that he was a marshal. And if he were a marshal, he would have told the truth. So, whichever way, he would have said that he and the other untied man were marshals.

Therefore, when the other untied man told the sheriff that the first man had said they were marshals, he was obviously telling the truth. But if he had been an outlaw, he would have lied. Thus, the sheriff knew the two untied men were indeed the marshals and the other two men were the outlaws.

## Caspuccio the bandit (page 110)

Caspuccio said, "You're going to cut off my head."

If the King said this was true, he would have to behead Caspuccio to *make* it true. But he had said that the bandit would be hanged for making a true statement. However, if Caspuccio were hanged, that would make his statement false— which would mean he should have been beheaded, making the statement true after all! So, the king could not decide whether the statement was true or false. He had to let Caspuccio go!

## The three musicians (page 112)

First, the two children rowed to the other side of the river. One of them got out of the boat, and the other rowed back.

The first musician then rowed the boat across. When he reached the other side, the child who was there got into the boat and rowed it back.

Next, the two children took the boat across the river again. Again, one of them stayed there while the other brought the boat back. The second musician then rowed across.

This was done one more time, until all three musicians and one child were across the river. The musicians paid the child, who then rowed back across the river to his friend.

## Abdul's journeys (page 114)

It was actually quicker for Abdul to walk than it was for him to go by truck and camel!

For the first journey, going half the distance by truck took one hour. This was ten times faster than Abdul could have walked. In other words, Abdul could have walked halfway in ten hours. Therefore, if his camel ride was twice as slow as walking, it must have taken twenty hours. So altogether, Abdul's first journey took twenty-one hours.

If Abdul could walk halfway in ten hours, it obviously took him twenty hours to walk the whole way. So his homeward journey, walking, took only twenty hours—one hour less than his first journey.

## The bad bears (page 115)

If Bruno is telling the truth when he says that he did not break the pot, then the other three statements are false. This means that Bobo is lying when he says Bilda broke the  pot. However, this makes Bilda's statement, that Bobo is lying, true. We know that three of the bears are lying, so there can't be two true statements.

Therefore, Bruno's statement must be false, which means he broke the honeypot. Thus, Boffin's claim that Bobo broke it is false. So is Bobo's claim that Bilda broke it. Bilda's statement that Bobo is lying is the true one.

## The Ping-Pong and the Biggie
(page 116)

The Ping-Pong rolled into a corner. Because the Biggie was ten times bigger than the Ping-Pong, it could not fit into as small an angle as the Ping-Pong, as shown below. The Ping-Pong stayed in the corner until the Biggie grew tired and left.

# Brain

The puzzles you are about to do are brain twisters! It may seem as if some of them are impossible to solve—but all of them can be solved. There are lots of clues, but you have to sort out all the clues. You have to think about what each clue really means. And you may have to fit them together in different ways to find the answer.

# Twisters

It is best to use pencil and paper, so that you can write all the clues down and keep them straight in your mind. In some cases, it will be a big help if you draw diagrams or pictures. In some cases, you can solve the puzzle by just crossing out clues, until the right answer suddenly pops out at you!

# A trip downtown

Shayla and her mother went downtown.
They rode the bus, because Shayla's father
had taken the car to work. They visited a doctor
and saw a movie about dinosaurs at the museum.

Shayla's father does not go to work on Saturday or Sunday.
The doctor's office is closed on Wednesday. The bus they
took makes mid-day runs only on Monday, Wednesday,
Friday, and Saturday. The museum shows a different movie
on Friday. What day did Shayla and her mother go
downtown?

(answer on page 134)

# Ginny and Sarah

Sarah is now the same age that Ginny was four years ago.
Four years ago, Ginny was twice as old as Sarah. Ginny is
now twelve. How old is Sarah?

(answer on page 134)

# Black and white kittens

Marilyn's cat has had a litter of kittens. Some are all black and some are all white. Each black kitten has the same number of white brothers and sisters as black ones. But each white kitten has twice as many black brothers and sisters as white ones. How many kittens are in the litter?

(answer on page 134)

# The new kids

A new family had moved into the neighborhood. When Mrs. Frisby, a neighbor, passed the house, she saw four children playing in the yard. She could tell they were brothers and sisters, for they all looked very much alike.

"My, what a nice, big family," she exclaimed. "What are your names and ages?"

"I'm Carl," said a boy. He pointed at a girl who stood beside him. This is Jennifer. I'm a year older than she is."

"I'm George," said another boy. "I'm a year younger than my sister Susie."

"I'll be eight next month," announced Jennifer. "I'm three years younger than Susie."

How old was each child?

(answer on page 134)

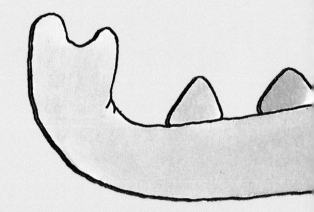

# The creatures of Zorp

On the planet Zorp, far off in another part of space, there are four kinds of creatures. Each kind of creature has a different number of legs.

- Whoofers have two more legs than Sizzles.

- Zompers have two more legs than Whoofers.

- Sizzles have two more legs than Yeeples.

- Yeeples have six fewer legs than Zompers.

How many legs does each kind of Zorpian creature have?

(answer on page 135)

# A hungry bookworm

Two large books are side by side on a shelf. The first book, on the left, contains two hundred pages. The second book contains one hundred pages.

A hungry bookworm got into the first book. It ate its way through the first page of the first book and all the way through the last page of the second book. How many pages (not counting the covers) did the bookworm eat through?

(answer on page 135)

# Three dogs

Three dogs were walking one behind the other. The dogs' names were Spot, Ginger, and Bingo. Spot was behind Bingo. Ginger was in front of Spot. Bingo was in front of Ginger. Which dog was first in line?

(answer on page 136)

# The great mouse race

Wheep, Squee, Eeper, Tweep, and Pweet are mice. Like all mice, they are fast runners. One day, the five mice decided to hold a race to see who was the fastest. When the race was over, here is how they finished:

- Wheep was not first.

- Pweet finished right behind Wheep.

- Squee was not second.

- Eeper came in two places after Squee.

- Tweep was not first or last.

Can you figure out the order in which the mice finished the race?

(answer on page 136)

# Swifty and Junior

To do this puzzle, you have to know some things about animals—such as, which animals have tails and which do not, and what kinds of animals are related to each other. For example, a dog is closely related to a wolf, but it is not very closely related to a bear.

Seven of the animals in a zoo are a tiger, a chimpanzee, a lioness and her cub, a leopard, and a spider monkey and her baby. One of the animals is named Swifty, and one is named Junior.

1. Swifty has a long tail.

2. The tiger is closely related to both Swifty and Junior.

3. Swifty has never touched Junior.

What kind of animal is Swifty?

(answer on page 137)

## A trip downtown (page 124)

Shayla's father does not work downtown on Saturday or Sunday. We know he was at work on this day, so Saturday and Sunday are ruled out. The doctor's office is closed on Wednesday, so Wednesday is out. The bus that Shayla and her mother want to take does not run in the middle of the day on Tuesday and Thursday, so these days are out. The museum does not show the dinosaur movie on Friday, but that is the movie Shayla and her mother saw. So, Friday is ruled out. This leaves only Monday.

## Ginny and Sarah (page 124)

Ginny is now twelve. Four years ago, she was eight. If Sarah is now the same age Ginny was four years ago, Sarah is now eight.

## Black and white kittens (page 125)

There are seven kittens in the litter—four black and three white. Each black kitten has three black and three white brothers and sisters. Each white kitten has two white and four black brothers and sisters.

## The new kids (page 125)

Jennifer announced that she would be eight next month, which means she is *now* seven. So, if she's three years younger than Susie, Susie is ten. Carl said he was a year older than Jennifer, so he is eight. And George, who is a year younger than Susie, must be nine.

## The creatures of Zorp (page 126)

The last clue tells us that Yeeples have six fewer legs than Zompers. So, we know a Zomper has at least six legs. The second clue tells us Zompers have two more legs than Whoofers, so Whoofers must have at least four legs. And the first clue told us Whoofers have two legs more than Sizzles, so Sizzles must have at least two legs.

However, clue three said that Sizzles have two more legs than Yeeples, meaning a Yeeple must have at least two legs. Therefore, to give a Sizzle two more legs than a Yeeple, we have to give it four legs. Then, we must add two legs to each of the other two creatures. That gives us:

- Zompers: 8 legs—two more than a Whoofer.
- Whoofers: 6 legs—two more than a Sizzle.
- Sizzles: 4 legs—two more than a Yeeple.
- Yeeples: 2 legs—six less than a Zomper.

## A hungry bookworm (page 128)

When two books are side by side on a shelf, the *front* cover of the first book, the book on the left, is pressed against the *back* cover of the second book. A book's first page is next to its front cover and its last page is next to its back cover. So, if the bookworm ate through the first page of the first book, it then ate its way through the book's front cover. Next, it ate its way through the back cover of the second book. Then it ate through the last page of the second book. So, altogether, it ate its way through only *two* pages.

## Three dogs (page 129)

The last two clues tell you that Ginger was in front of Spot and Bingo was in front of Ginger. So, Bingo was first, followed by Ginger, then Spot.

## The great mouse race (page 131)

We know that Wheep was not first. Pweet finished right behind Wheep, so she could not have been first, either. Eeper came in two places after Squee, so obviously he was not first. And Tweep was neither first nor last. That leaves only Squee. Squee was the winner.

If Squee was first, and we know that Eeper came in two places after her, then Eeper must have come in third.

We know that Pweet finished right behind Wheep. If Wheep had finished second, that would mean that Pweet had finished third. But from what we have worked out, we know that Eeper was third. So, Wheep could not have come in second. He had to have come in fourth. And, if Pweet was behind him, she must have been fifth. Tweep, then, had to have been second.

So, the order of finish in the Great Mouse Race was:

1. Squee
2. Tweep
3. Eeper
4. Wheep
5. Pweet

## Swifty and Junior (page 132)

Clue 1 says that Swifty has a long tail. That rules out the chimpanzee, for chimpanzees do not have a tail.

Clue 2 says the tiger is closely related to both Swifty and Junior. So, the tiger can't be Swifty or Junior. This clue also rules out the spider monkey and her baby. Tigers, lions, and leopards are close relatives. They are all cats. But monkeys and apes are primates—a very different kind of animal. So, we know that Swifty is either the lioness, her cub, or the leopard.

Clue 3 tells us that Swifty has never touched Junior. We know that the lioness and her cub must touch one another often, so neither of them can be Swifty. That leaves only the leopard.

# ■Look

The next few puzzles have shapes for you to look at and think about. You are asked to figure out things. How would a certain shape look if it were turned around? Or, how many shapes are there inside another shape?

# and Think

There are no clues for puzzles of this kind. They are much like jigsaw puzzles without pieces. To solve them, you have to be able to see in your mind how things fit together, and how shapes can be put together to make other shapes. Many people find this sort of thing very difficult. For some people, it's easy and lots of fun. Let's see how it is for you.

# Seeing squares

How many squares do you see?

(answer on page 148)

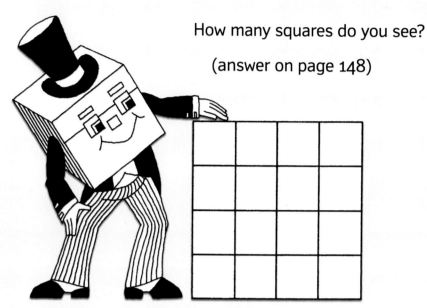

# Seeing triangles

This square has been divided into triangles.
How many triangles can you find?

(answer on page 148)

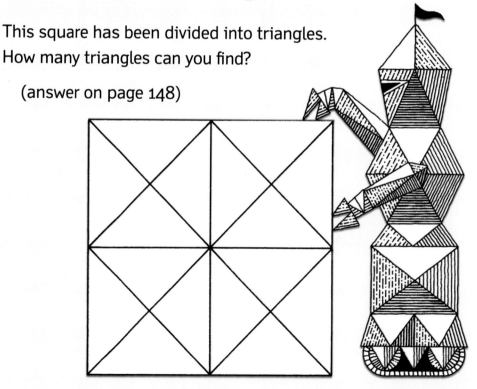

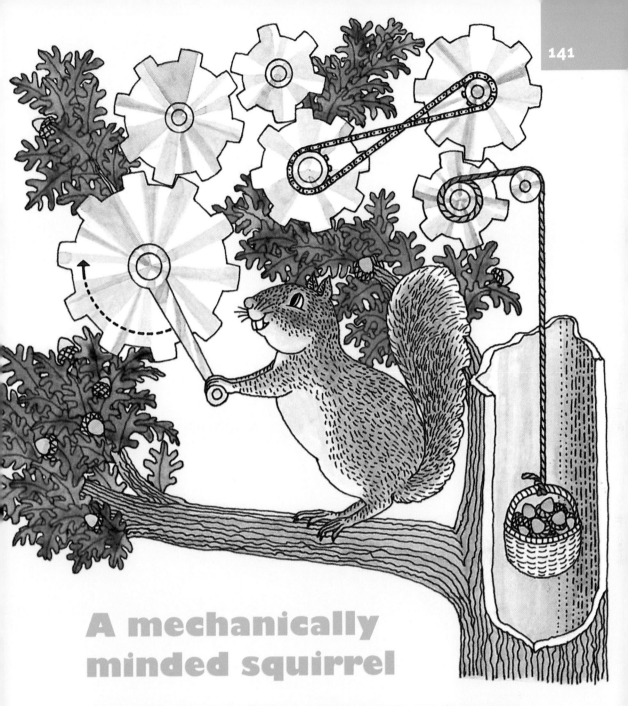

# A mechanically minded squirrel

If you can figure out which way each gear is moving, you can tell whether the squirrel is pulling the basket of acorns *up* or letting it *down*. The first gear is turning in the direction of the dotted arrow. Here is a hint to get you started: the second gear will turn in the opposite direction.

(answer on page 149)

# Hidden sides

1. No matter how you look at a cube, such as a building block, you can see only three sides of it. How many sides (including top and bottom) does a cube have altogether?

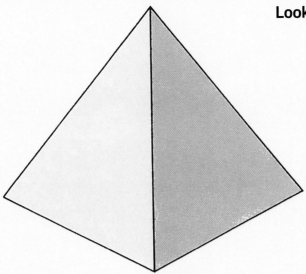

2. How many sides, including the bottom, does this pyramid
have? Here is a hint—the back of the pyramid looks just
like the front.

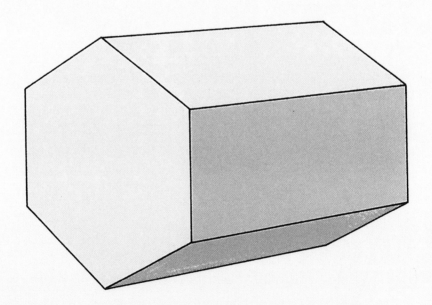

3. How many sides, including top and bottom, does this
shape have? The back looks just like the front.

(answers on page 149)

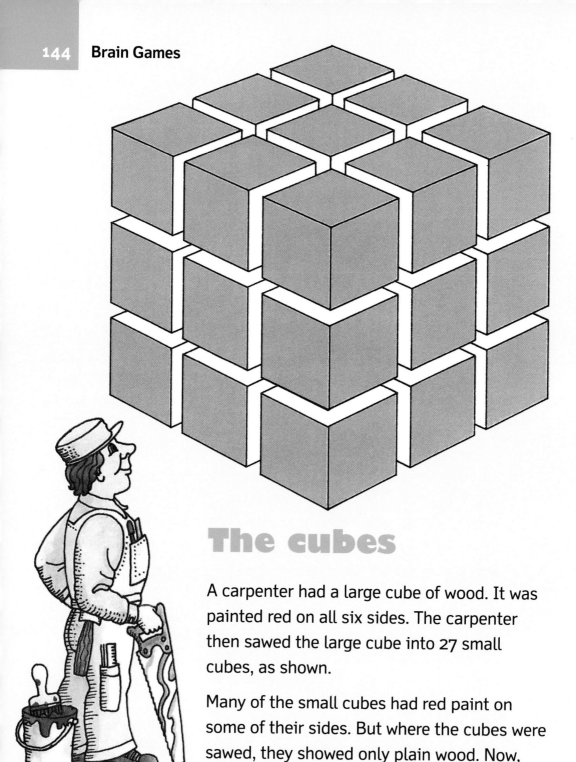

# The cubes

A carpenter had a large cube of wood. It was painted red on all six sides. The carpenter then sawed the large cube into 27 small cubes, as shown.

Many of the small cubes had red paint on some of their sides. But where the cubes were sawed, they showed only plain wood. Now, put your imagination to work and see if you can figure out the answers to these questions:

1. How many of the small cubes had red paint on 3 sides?

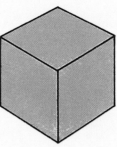

2. How many of the small cubes had red paint on 2 sides?

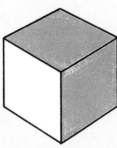

3. How many of the small cubes had red paint on only 1 side?

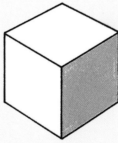

4. Were there any of the small cubes that had no paint on them at all?

(answers on page 149)

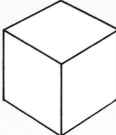

# Kliggs, klaggs, and kluggs

1. Let's call this shape a "kligg." This is one side of a kligg:

Now try to turn the kligg around in your mind. Which one of the drawings below shows the other side of a kligg?

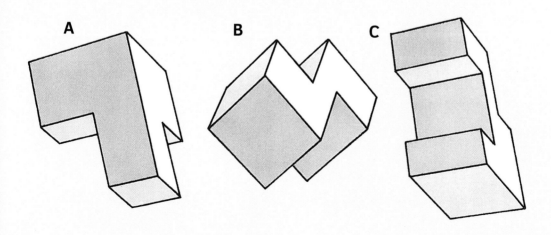

A      B      C

2. Let's call this shape a "klagg."
   This is one side of a klagg:

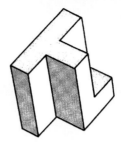

Now try to turn the klagg around in your mind. Which one of the drawings below shows the other side of a klagg?

A 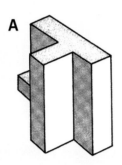  B 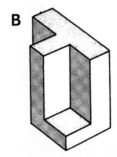  C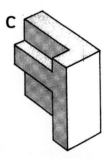

3. Let's call this shape a "klugg."
   This is one side of a klugg:

Now try to turn the klugg around in your mind. Which one of the drawings below shows the other side of a klugg?

(answers on page 149)

A 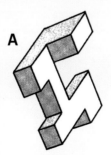  B 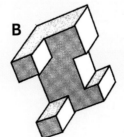  C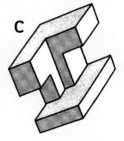

## Seeing squares (page 140)

There is 1 large square with 16 small squares inside it, making 17. But …

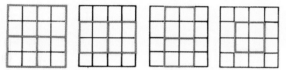

the small squares can be combined like this to make 9 more squares, or a total of 26 squares. And …

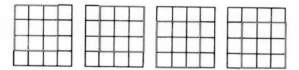

the small squares can be combined in other ways to form 4 slightly larger squares. So, altogether, there are 30 squares.

## Seeing triangles (page 140)

There are 44 triangles in all, as shown below.

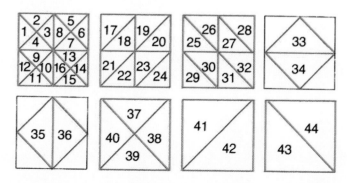

# A mechanically minded squirrel

(page 141)

The arrows show the direction in which each gear is moving. The last gear is moving counterclockwise—turning toward its left— so it is pulling the basket up.

## Hidden sides (pages 142-143)

1. A cube has six sides, including the top and bottom.

2. A pyramid has five sides, including the bottom.

3. This shape has eight sides, including the top and bottom.

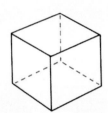 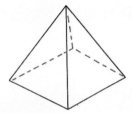 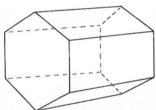

## The cubes (pages 144-145)

1. Eight cubes have red paint on three sides.

2. Twelve cubes have red paint on two sides.

3. Six cubes have red paint on one side.

4. Only one cube has no paint on it at all.

## Kliggs, klaggs, and kluggs (pages 146-147)

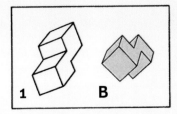 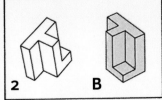 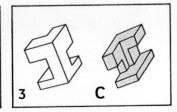

# Wordles

As you have probably guessed, these puzzles are word puzzles. They ask you to find hidden words, take words apart and rearrange them, solve codes, and so on. You will need a pencil and paper so that you can write things down.

To solve these puzzles, it helps if you know lots of words and their meanings. If you do a lot of reading, these puzzles should be fairly easy—and lots of fun.

# Turnaround words

When you spell most words backwards, you get a word that doesn't mean anything, such as girl—lrig. But sometimes when you turn a word around, you get a new, real word. For example, spell *rat* backwards and you get *tar*.

Here are clues to some words that become new words when they are turned around. See how many you can get.

1. Turn around a word for a number and get a word for something with which you catch fish.

2. Turn around a word for a tool to cook with and get a word for something a baby often does.

3. Turn around a word that means "at this very moment" and get a word that means "gained by a victory."

4. Turn around the word for a thing you do work with and get the word for something pirates were always seeking.

5. Turn around a word that means "not dead," and get a word that means "very, very bad."

6. Turn around a word for someone who isn't truthful and you'll get a word for something a train needs.

(answers on page 162)

# Beheaded words

To behead a word, you chop off the first letter. Sometimes when you do this, you get a brand-new word.

Here is a puzzle that gives you clues to words that change into other words when they are beheaded. For example— behead the word that means the opposite of closed, and you will get the word that means a place where pigs are kept, or a tool to write with. The word is *open*. When you behead it, you get *pen*.

Ready? Go.

1. Behead the word that means "a sandy place by water" and you will get the word that means "every single one."

2. Behead the word for what you think with and you will get the word for falling water.

3. Behead the word for a scare and you will get the word that is the opposite of wrong.

4. Behead the word for a precious metal and you will get the word for something that has been around a long time.

5. Behead the word for a tool that helps you reach a high place and you will get the name of a poisonous snake.

6. Behead the word that means "to make a hole" and you will get the word for the material that metal comes from.

(answers on page 162)

# A wordy dinosaur

Have you ever tried to see how many words you could make using the letters in just one word? For example, using the four letters in the little word **door,** you can make four other words: **do, or, rod,** and **odor.**

The word **dinosaur** has twice as many letters as **door,** but you can make a lot more than just twice as many words from them. It is possible to make at least 50 different words from the letters in **dinosaur!**

See how many words you can make. If you can get from 40 to 50, you're a Supergenius, Top Grade! From 30 to 39 makes you a Genius, Junior Class. From 20 to 29, you're a Whizzbang. And from 10 to 19, you're Pretty Smart.

(answers on page 162)

# Changeover

Changeover is a game in which you change a word, one letter at a time, until you have a word that means the opposite of the word you started with. However, each time you change a letter, you must have a *real* word. Here's how to change **some** to **none** in three moves.

1. Change **some** to **come** by changing **s** to **c**.

2. Change **come** to **cone** by changing **m** to **n**.

3. Change **cone** to **none** by changing **c** to **n**.

And so, you have gone from some to none—a complete changeover! Now, try these changeovers on your own.

1. Change **glee** to **glum** in two moves.

2. Change **hill** to **vale** in three moves.

3. Change **more** to **less** in four moves.

4. Change **cold** to **heat** in four moves.

5. Change **hard** to **soft** in six moves.

(answers on page 163)

# Strange lands

Five children who were traveling with their parents met at an airport. Although they all came from different countries, they found they all spoke the same language. But, just for fun, each child scrambled up the name of his or her country so the others would have to figure out what the real name was.

- Joe said he was from Andaca.

- Gail came from Duneti Testas.

- Molly was from Clonstad.

- Juanita came from an island called Turpeo Crio.

- Peter proudly stated he was from Tiasalura.

By rearranging the letters of each name, you can find out where each child was really from.

(answers on page 163)

# The pup's tale

A number of words in English read the same backwards as forwards. One such word, for example, is *toot*. Another is *bib*, the cloth a baby wears under its chin when it eats.

A word that reads the same backwards or forwards is called a palindrome *(PAL ihn drohm)*. See how many palindromes you can find in the following story:

The police had been called. The Smiths' family pet, a collie pup, had been stolen!

"Ailia took him for a walk at noon," said Mom, pointing to her little girl. "She stopped to buy a bottle of pop. When she turned around, the dog was gone."

The little girl was crying bitterly. Tears poured from each eye, and her face was redder than a radish.

"I wonder who did such a deed?" muttered the policeman. "I will level with you; only a real dud would steal from such a tiny tot!"

"Wow!" Dad suddenly cried. "Look!"

There in the yard was the dog. It hadn't been stolen at all, just lost. And it had found its way home like an airplane following a radar signal!

(answer on page 163)

# All kinds of codes

Here are some secret messages to decode. Once you have figured out how each code works, you can use it with your friends.

1. In this message, numbers are obviously used for letters. Here is a hint: everything is in the proper order.

   4 5 3 15 4 9 14 7   9 19   6 21 14

2. Look very carefully at this message:

   ITI SALLIN HO WYO ULOO KATIT

3. The clue for this message is: *backwards.*

   GSV ZOKSZYVG RH GFIMVW ZILFMW

4. This one is much harder, because you have to decode it twice. Here's a hint: This code combines two of the other codes. After you decode it once, look at it carefully.

   HKZ XVWW RUUV IVMGO BZMWYZ XPDZ IWH

(answers on page 164)

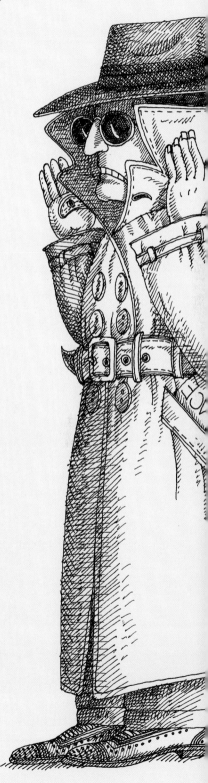

# Animal, vegetable, mineral

Have you ever played the game called "Animal, Vegetable, or Mineral"? One person thinks of something that is animal, vegetable, or mineral. Then another person tries to find what it is by asking 20 questions.

Here is a different kind of animal, vegetable, mineral game. It is made up of twelve scrambled words. Four words are the names of things that belong to the animal kingdom, four belong to the vegetable kingdom, and four belong to the mineral kingdom. (Minerals are the lifeless things that come out of the earth, such as metals, rocks, and jewels.) The names aren't in any order. There is a clue with each, to help you figure out what it is. But the clues are tricky!

1. NOFWESRUL

   It likes sunshine.

2. DALREEM

   It's bright green.

3. GRAASUPSA

   It looks like a little tree.

4. BLUEBEMEB

   You may find one in your backyard.

5. OPREDLA

   It's orange and black.

6. TAINREG

You see it on many buildings.

7. DODMINA

Some people say it's their best friend.

8. HYNTOP

It's sometimes in trees.

9. NPKUPMI

It sometimes wears a face.

10. LUTTER

It has a hard shell.

11. PROCEP

It's shiny orange at first, but turns brown as it gets old.

12. ETEB

It's hard and red.

(answers on page 165)

## Wordies
# Answers

## Turnaround words (pages 152-153)

1. ten—net
2. pan—nap
3. now—won

4. tool—loot
5. live—evil
6. liar—rail

## Beheaded words (page 154)

1. beach; each
2. brain; rain
3. fright; right

4. gold; old
5. ladder; adder
6. bore; ore

## A wordy dinosaur (page 155)

Here, in alphabetical order, are 50 words you can make using the letters in **dinosaur**. It is possible to make even more words, but most of them are not very common.

| | | | | |
|---|---|---|---|---|
| adorn | don | nod | rind | sin |
| aid | dour | nor | road | sir |
| air | drain | oar | roan | so |
| an | dun | on | rod | soar |
| and | duo | or | ruin | sod |
| as | in | our | run | soda |
| dais | ion | raid | sad | son |
| darn | iron | rain | said | sour |
| din | is | ran | sand | sun |
| do | no | rid | sari | us |

## Changeover (page 156)

1. Change **glee** to **glue** and **glue** to **glum**.

2. Change **hill** to **hall**; **hall** to **hale** (which means healthy); and **hale** to **vale** (a small valley).

3. Change **more** to **lore** (stories about a certain subject); **lore** to **lose**; **lose** to **loss**; and **loss** to **less**.

4. Change **cold** to **hold**; **hold** to **held**; **held** to **head**; and **head** to **heat**.

5. Change **hard** to **card**; **card** to **cart**; **cart** to **part**; **part** to **port**; **port** to **sort**; and **sort** to **soft**.

## Strange lands (page 157)

Andaca is Canada.

Duneti Testas is the United States.

Clonstad is Scotland.

Turpeo Crio is Puerto Rico.

Tiasalura is Australia.

## The pup's tale (page 158)

There are 15 different palindromes in the story. In the order in which they appear, they are:

| | | | | |
|---|---|---|---|---|
| pup | mom | redder | level | wow |
| ailia | pop | did | dud | dad |
| noon | eye | deed | tot | radar |

## All kinds of codes (page 159)

1. Numbers are used for letters in proper alphabetical order. Thus, 1 is A, 2 is B, and so on. So, the message reads:

    4  5  3 15   4  9 14 7   9 19    6 21 14

    D E C O D I N G   I S   F U N

2. If you looked carefully, you saw that the message is made up of ordinary words that are just spaced differently:

    ITI SALLIN HO WYO ULOO KATIT

    IT IS ALL IN HOW YOU LOOK AT IT

3. The letters of the alphabet have been turned around so that A is Z, B is Y, and so on:

    GSV ZOKSZYVG RH GFIMVW ZILFMW

    THE ALPHABET IS TURNED AROUND

4. If you realized that this, too, is a backwards alphabet, as in (3), you decoded it and got:

    HKZ XVWW RUUV IVMGO BZMWYZ XPZD  IWH

    SPA  CEDD  IFFE  RENTL YANDBA CKWA RDS

    Then, if you looked at it carefully, as the clue suggested, you saw that it was just ordinary words spaced differently, as in (2).

    SPA  CEDD  IFFE  RENTL YANDBA CKWA  RDS

    SPACED  DIFFERENTLY  AND  BACKWARDS

# Animal, vegetable, mineral

(pages 160-161)

1. NOFWESRUL—SUNFLOWER (vegetable)

2. DALREEM—EMERALD (mineral)

3. GRAASUPSA—ASPARAGUS (vegetable)

4. BLUEBEMEB—BUMBLEBEE (animal)

5. OPREDLA—LEOPARD (animal)

6. TAINREG—GRANITE (mineral)

7. DODMINA—DIAMOND (mineral)

8. HYNTOP—PYTHON (animal)

9. NPKUPMI—PUMPKIN (vegetable)

10. LUTTER—TURTLE (animal)

11. PROCEP—COPPER (mineral)

12. ETEB—BEET (vegetable)

# +Arithme-

Many people like puzzles that use numbers. In other words, arithmetic puzzles. However, these puzzles are nothing like the plain old arithmetic problems you do for homework. Many of these puzzles are really jokes and tricks—arithmetricks! They're fun!

You will need a pencil and paper for most of these puzzles, of course. And you will have to know how to do some addition, subtraction, and multiplication. But most of all, you must read carefully and use common sense. Many of these puzzles are easier than they seem, but they are tricky.

# Tricks

Some of the puzzles ask you to figure out how many of something somebody started with. But all you are told is how many they finished with. Here is an important hint for solving such puzzles: work backwards. That is, take the last number the puzzle gives and start subtracting or adding as needed. In this way, you can work back to the starting number.

# Nimble numbers

1. When you add 10 to 100, you get 110. When you multiply 100 by 10, you get 1,000—a lot more. But what number makes a larger number when you *add* it to 100 than when you multiply it by 100?

2. What three numbers make the same number when they are multiplied as when they are added?

3. How can you make three 1's equal 12?

   1 1 1

4. How can you make four 7's equal 78?

   7 7 7 7

5. How much is double one-half of three-quarters?

   (answers on page 186)

# The garage sale

Mrs. Wuggins went to a garage sale in her neighborhood. She bought an old lamp and a handmade rug. She paid a total of $5.25 for both of these things. The rug cost 25 cents more than the lamp. How much did each thing cost?

(answers on page 186)

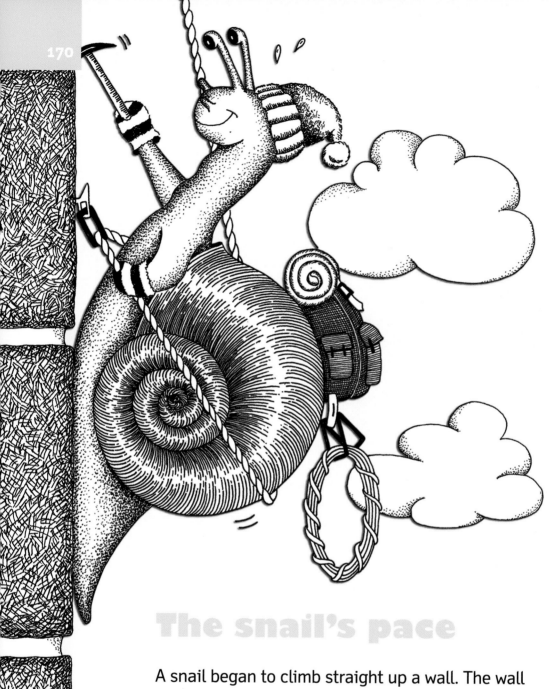

## The snail's pace

A snail began to climb straight up a wall. The wall was made of bricks and was exactly 24 bricks high. The snail climbed up three bricks each day. But each night it slid back two bricks.

How many days did it take the snail to reach the top of the wall?

(answer on page 186)

# The explorers

Two explorers, a man and a woman, were making their way through a thick jungle. When they had to wade through a river, many of their food packages were spoiled. They divided the remaining packages into two equal shares and continued on their way.

By the time the explorers reached civilization, each one had eaten five food packages. The total number of packages left was the same number each explorer had started with.

How many food packages had the explorers divided?

(answer on page 187)

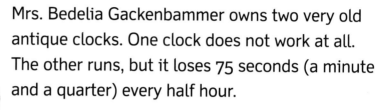

# The antique clocks

Mrs. Bedelia Gackenbammer owns two very old antique clocks. One clock does not work at all. The other runs, but it loses 75 seconds (a minute and a quarter) every half hour.

If both clocks are set at twelve o'clock midnight on a Sunday, which one will show the right time most often during the next ten days?

(answer on page 187)

# The Klucksburg clock

The town clock of Klucksburg strikes each hour with a deep *bong*. Each bong lasts one second. The time between two bongs is one-fourth of a second. It takes the clock six seconds to strike five o'clock. How long does it take it to strike nine o'clock?

(answer on page 188)

# A square triangle

The numbers 3, 6, and 10 are sometimes called triangular numbers. That's because if you show them as balls, you can arrange each group of balls in the shape of a triangle:

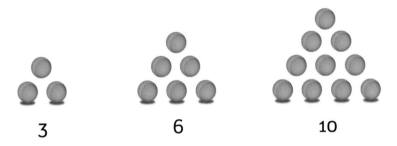

3          6          10

The numbers 4, 9, and 16 are sometimes called square numbers. That's because if you show them as balls, the balls can be arranged in the shape of a square:

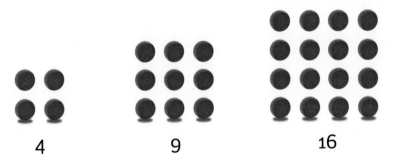

4          9          16

Many other numbers (past 2) can also be shown as either triangles or squares. But some numbers are both. What is the lowest number that can be shown as *both* a triangle and a square?

(answer on page 188)

# The Dobbs children

The Dobbs children were all out playing in their backyard. All their pet dogs and cats were in the yard with them. When Mr. Dobbs looked out the window, he saw, counting children, dogs, and cats, seven heads and twenty-two legs. How many children were playing in the yard?

(answer on page 188)

# Growing younger?

Ellen's father is now five times older than she is. But he told her that in five more years, he'll only be *three* times as old as she will be then. Is this possible? (You will have to do a little arithmetic to find out.)

(answer on page 189)

# The stolen banana

A small monkey stole a banana from a big monkey and ran away with it. The small monkey ran 14 steps before the big monkey saw what had happened. Then the big monkey chased the small one. For every 10 steps the little monkey ran, the big monkey took 5 steps, but these 5 steps were equal to 12 of the little monkey's steps.

How many steps will the little monkey take before the big monkey catches up to it?

(answer on page 189)

# Bread for wood

Three goblins, named Snurf, Snagga, and Guff, lived in a clearing in a woods. Each goblin had his own small but cozy house.

One cold winter day, Snurf and Snagga went out to get fire-wood. Guff stayed home to bake bread. The three had agreed to divide the firewood evenly. Guff would pay for his share with loaves of bread.

Snurf found a long log. He cut it into five pieces, each as long as he was. Snagga found a shorter log. He cut it into three pieces, each as long as he was. Because the goblins were exactly the same size, the pieces of wood were all the same size.

Snurf and Snagga brought their wood home. They saw they could not divide eight pieces three ways, of course. But they cut each piece into three pieces, so that there were twenty-four altogether— making eight for each of them. Guff gave them eight loaves of bread to pay for his eight pieces.

However, Snurf and Snagga disagreed on how to divide the loaves. Snurf felt he should get more than Snagga because he had brought home more wood. How can Snurf and Snagga divide the loaves fairly?

(answer on page 189)

# Do you sudoku?

Sudoku is a kind of number puzzle, but you don't use arithmetic to solve it. That is, you do not add, subtract, or multiply. Instead, you use *reasoning* (thinking) to solve the puzzle.

A sudoku puzzle is shaped like a grid—a large box filled with squares going across in rows, down in columns, and forming smaller boxes inside the large box. Some sudoku puzzles have 16 squares, with 4 columns across and 4 rows down. Every row and column is divided into 4 squares and each small box contains 4 squares. Some puzzles have 36 squares. These are a little harder to solve. Still other puzzles have 81 squares. These are the hardest of all. Start out with a couple of 16-square sudoku puzzles. After you have figured those out, challenge yourself with the harder ones.

A 16-square sudoku puzzle uses the numbers 1, 2, 3, and 4. A 36-square puzzle uses the numbers 1 through 6, and an 81-square puzzle uses the numbers 1 through 9. Some of the numbers in the puzzle are already filled in. Your job is to figure out what numbers go in the other squares. In a 16-square sudoku puzzle, for example, each row, column, and dark-lined box must use all the numbers 1 through 4, using each number only once.

How do you solve a sudoku puzzle? Use the numbers that are already shown. If a row contains the numbers 4 and 1, you cannot use 4 or 1 again in that row. The more squares you fill in, the easier it gets to figure out the numbers for the other squares. You may want to draw the sudoku puzzles on the next three pages onto a piece of scrap paper. That way, you can try different numbers in the boxes and erase the ones that don't work.

(answers on page 190)

# Easy

1

| | 4 | | 1 |
|---|---|---|---|
| 1 | | | 3 |
| 2 | | | 4 |
| 4 | | 3 | |

2

| | | 2 | 4 |
|---|---|---|---|
| | | | |
| | | | |
| 1 | 2 | | |

# Medium

**3**

| | 4 | | | 6 | |
|---|---|---|---|---|---|
| | | | 4 | | |
| | 5 | | 1 | | |
| | | 3 | | 5 | |
| 3 | 5 | | | | |
| | 1 | | | 3 | |

**4**

| | | | 4 | 6 | |
|---|---|---|---|---|---|
| | | | | | 5 |
| | | | | | 2 |
| 5 | | 4 | | | 1 |
| 4 | | | | | |
| | 5 | 2 | | | |

# Hard

5

6

# Can you KenKen®?

KenKen® puzzles are also number puzzles. But unlike in sudoku, to solve a KenKen® puzzle you have to add or subtract. In harder KenKen® puzzles, you may have to multiply or divide.

Just like sudoku, KenKen® puzzles are based on a grid. You may have a grid of 9 squares, with 3 rows across and 3 columns down; 16 squares, with 4 rows across and 4 columns down; or 36 squares, with 6 rows across and 6 columns down. And, just like in a sudoku puzzle, you have to fill in the missing numbers, using each number only once in a row or column. But in a KenKen® puzzle, dark-outlined shapes inside the grid contain clues about the numbers that belong in those squares. The small number in a dark-outlined shape tells you what the total of the numbers in the shape should be. The sign (plus or minus) tells you what you have to do to get that total (add or subtract). An outlined one-box shape is a "freebie"—it gives you the number that belongs in that box.

Look at the first puzzle on the next page. This puzzle has 3 rows across and 3 columns down. That tells you that you can only use the numbers 1, 2, and 3. There are no signs in the dark-outlined shapes of these two puzzles. They are both addition puzzles, so add to get the totals shown in each outlined shape. A good way to start is to write in any freebie numbers first. This puzzle has one freebie, the outlined box at the top of the third column with the number 1 in it. Now you know that the top row and the third column cannot have another 1. Just like with the sudoku puzzles, copy the KenKens® onto a sheet of paper and try different numbers until you find the right ones. After you have solved the addition puzzles, try one in which you have to both add and subtract.

(answers on page 191)

# Easy

1

| 3 | 5 | 1 |
|---|---|---|
|   |   | 5 |
| 4 |   |   |

2

| 5 | 5 |   | 4 |
|---|---|---|---|
|   | 3 | 4 |   |
| 5 |   | 4 | 3 |
|   | 7 |   |   |

## Medium

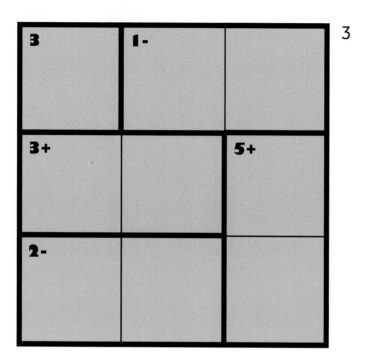

3

3 | 1- |
3+ | | 5+
2- | |

4

3 | 1- | | 7+
3+ | 9+ | |
| | 5+ |
4 | 1- | | 1

## Hard

5

| 1- |  | 6+ | 2- |  |
|----|----|----|----|----|
| 4 | 6+ |  | 3 | 3+ |
| 2- |  | 1- |  |  |
|  | 1- | 1 | 3- |  |
| 2 |  | 6+ |  | 4 |

6

| 3+ |  | 1- | 5 | 3- |  |
|----|----|----|----|----|----|
| 11+ | 5- |  | 1- |  | 1- |
|  |  | 2 | 1- | 7+ |  |
| 1- | 5 | 7+ |  |  | 6 |
|  | 1- |  | 3+ |  | 1- |
| 2 |  | 11+ |  | 1 |  |

## Nimble numbers (page 168)

1. The number 1. When you multiply 100 by 1, you get 100. But when you add 1 to 100, you get 101.

2. The numbers 1, 2, and 3: $1 + 2 + 3 = 6$ and $1 \times 2 \times 3 = 6$.

3. Arrange the three 1's this way: $11 + 1 = 12$.

4. Arrange the four 7's this way: $77 + 7/7 = 78$. (7/7—seven-sevenths— is equal to 1.)

5. Double one-half of three-quarters is three-quarters. Twice one-half of any number is the whole number.

## The garage sale (page 169)

Subtract the 25 cents difference from the total and get $5.00. Half of this is $2.50. So, Mrs. Wuggins paid $2.50 for the lamp and $2.75 for the rug.

## The snail's pace (page 170)

It took the snail 22 days. If the snail climbs three bricks a day and slips back two bricks each night, it is actually gaining one brick a day. So, after 21 nights, the snail had climbed 21 bricks. The next day, it climbed the last three bricks and reached the top of the wall.

## The explorers (page 171)

The explorers divided the remaining food packages equally. In other words, each explorer had *half* the packages.

When they got to civilization, the number of packages they had left equaled the number each had started with. So, if each started with half the packages, the number left must equal half of the total they divided.

If half the packages were left, the explorers must have eaten the other half. We know they each ate five, which would be a total of ten, or half of what they started with. So, half of the total number must be ten. Therefore, they divided twenty packages.

## The antique clocks (page 172)

The clock that doesn't work will show the right time twenty times during the next ten days—at twelve noon and twelve midnight each day. The clock that runs, but loses time, won't show the right time *at all* during the next ten days!

The clock that runs loses 75 seconds every half hour. This works out to one-half hour every twelve hours. Thus, at twelve noon on Monday, this clock will show eleven-thirty. At midnight Monday it will show eleven o'clock. And each day after that, it gets farther off.

This clock actually won't show the right time for twelve days. It will have lost twelve hours in twelve days, so it will finally show twelve o'clock at midnight on the twelfth day.

### The Klucksburg clock (page 172)

It takes exactly eleven seconds for the clock to strike nine. There are nine one-second bongs. And, there are eight quarter-seconds, or a total of two seconds, between bongs.

### A square triangle (page 173)

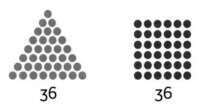

36        36

### The Dobbs children (page 174)

Mr. Dobbs counted seven heads, so you know the number of dogs, cats, and children must add up to seven. And as the puzzle said there were dogs and cats, you know there must be *at least* two dogs and two cats. Four animals and three children would account for the seven heads Mr. Dobbs counted.

Two dogs and two cats, with four legs each, would account for sixteen legs (4 x 4 = 16). Three children, with two legs each, account for six legs (3 x 2 = 6). And 16 + 6 = 22, the number of legs Mr. Dobbs counted. So there were three children playing in the backyard.

## Growing younger? (page 174)

Pick any number for Ellen's age. Multiply it by five to get her father's age. Then add five to both numbers to see if one is now three times the other. It may take you several tries to find that if Ellen is five, her father has to be twenty-five, five times older. In five years, then, Ellen will be ten and her father will be thirty, or three times older.

## The stolen banana (page 175)

The little monkey will be caught by its 84th step.

The little monkey starts out 14 steps ahead. Then the big monkey starts to chase it. As the little monkey runs 10 steps, the big monkey runs 5 steps that are equal to 12 of the little monkey's steps. So, at this point, the little monkey has run 24 steps and the big monkey is 12 steps behind.

From then on, for every 10 steps the little monkey takes, the big monkey gains 2 steps. When the small monkey has run 34 steps, the big one is 10 steps behind. At 44 steps for the small monkey, the big one is 8 behind. When the little monkey has run 74 steps, the big one is only 2 behind. The big monkey will catch the little one after it has taken 10 more steps.

## Bread for wood (pages 176-177)

Snurf should get 7 loaves and Snagga should get 1 loaf.

The 5 pieces of wood Snurf brought home were cut into 15 pieces. Snurf kept 8 pieces, which means he gave away 7. The 3 pieces of wood Snagga brought were cut into 9 pieces. So, because Snagga kept 8 pieces, he gave away only one.

**Do you sudoku?** (pages 178-181)

**1**

| 3 | 4 | 2 | 1 |
|---|---|---|---|
| 1 | 2 | 4 | 3 |
| 2 | 3 | 1 | 4 |
| 4 | 1 | 3 | 2 |

**2**

| 3 | 1 | 2 | 4 |
|---|---|---|---|
| 2 | 4 | 3 | 1 |
| 4 | 3 | 1 | 2 |
| 1 | 2 | 4 | 3 |

**3**

| 5 | 4 | 1 | 3 | 6 | 2 |
|---|---|---|---|---|---|
| 3 | 6 | 2 | 4 | 1 | 5 |
| 4 | 5 | 6 | 1 | 2 | 3 |
| 1 | 2 | 3 | 6 | 5 | 4 |
| 6 | 3 | 5 | 2 | 4 | 1 |
| 2 | 1 | 4 | 5 | 3 | 6 |

**4**

| 2 | 1 | 5 | 4 | 6 | 3 |
|---|---|---|---|---|---|
| 3 | 4 | 6 | 1 | 2 | 5 |
| 1 | 6 | 3 | 5 | 4 | 2 |
| 5 | 2 | 4 | 6 | 3 | 1 |
| 4 | 3 | 1 | 2 | 5 | 6 |
| 6 | 5 | 2 | 3 | 1 | 4 |

**5**

| 8 | 7 | 1 | 2 | 5 | 3 | 9 | 4 | 6 |
|---|---|---|---|---|---|---|---|---|
| 9 | 2 | 5 | 7 | 4 | 6 | 8 | 1 | 3 |
| 4 | 6 | 3 | 1 | 8 | 9 | 5 | 2 | 7 |
| 7 | 4 | 2 | 6 | 1 | 8 | 3 | 9 | 5 |
| 5 | 3 | 8 | 9 | 2 | 7 | 4 | 6 | 1 |
| 1 | 9 | 6 | 5 | 3 | 4 | 2 | 7 | 8 |
| 2 | 8 | 7 | 4 | 6 | 5 | 1 | 3 | 9 |
| 3 | 1 | 9 | 8 | 7 | 2 | 6 | 5 | 4 |
| 6 | 5 | 4 | 3 | 9 | 1 | 7 | 8 | 2 |

**6**

| 4 | 3 | 1 | 9 | 6 | 2 | 5 | 7 | 8 |
|---|---|---|---|---|---|---|---|---|
| 2 | 5 | 7 | 3 | 8 | 4 | 1 | 9 | 6 |
| 6 | 8 | 9 | 1 | 7 | 5 | 4 | 3 | 2 |
| 7 | 2 | 4 | 5 | 9 | 3 | 8 | 6 | 1 |
| 3 | 6 | 8 | 7 | 4 | 1 | 9 | 2 | 5 |
| 1 | 9 | 5 | 8 | 2 | 6 | 7 | 4 | 3 |
| 9 | 4 | 3 | 2 | 5 | 8 | 6 | 1 | 7 |
| 8 | 1 | 6 | 4 | 3 | 7 | 2 | 5 | 9 |
| 5 | 7 | 2 | 6 | 1 | 9 | 3 | 8 | 4 |

## Can you KenKen®? (pages 182-185)

**1**

| 3   2 | 5   3 | 1   1 |
|---|---|---|
| 1 | 2 | 5   3 |
| 4   3 | 2 | 1 |

**2**

| 5   1 | 5   3 | 2 | 4   4 |
|---|---|---|---|
| 4 | 3   2 | 4   1 | 3 |
| 5   3 | 1 | 4   4 | 3   2 |
| 2 | 7   4 | 3 | 1 |

**3**

| 3   3 | 1-   2 | 1 |
|---|---|---|
| 3+   2 | 1 | 5+   3 |
| 2-   1 | 3 | 2 |

**4**

| 3   3 | 1-   2 | 1 | 7+   4 |
|---|---|---|---|
| 3+   2 | 9+   1 | 4 | 3 |
| 1 | 4 | 5+   3 | 2 |
| 4   4 | 1-   3 | 2 | 1   1 |

**5**

| 1-   1 | 2 | 6+   4 | 2-   5 | 3 |
|---|---|---|---|---|
| 4   4 | 6+   5 | 2 | 3   3 | 3+   1 |
| 2-   5 | 1 | 1-   3 | 4 | 2 |
| 3 | 1-   4 | 1   1 | 3-   2 | 5 |
| 2   2 | 3 | 6+   5 | 1 | 4   4 |

**6**

| 3+   1 | 2 | 1-   4 | 5   5 | 3-   6 | 3 |
|---|---|---|---|---|---|
| 11+   6 | 5-   1 | 3 | 1-   4 | 5 | 1-   2 |
| 5 | 6 | 2   2 | 1-   3 | 7+   4 | 1 |
| 1-   4 | 5   5 | 7+   1 | 2 | 3 | 6   6 |
| 3 | 1-   4 | 6 | 3+   1 | 2 | 1-   5 |
| 2   2 | 3 | 11+   5 | 6 | 1   1 | 4 |

**Brain**

# Busters

These puzzles are just like some of the puzzles you have already done, except that they are **harder.** Some of them are simply trickier Arithmetricks, some are more ponderous Ponderers, some are twistier Brain Twisters. You go about solving them the same way you solved the other puzzles. However, you will have to work a lot harder—but, of course, that is where the fun comes in!

# Who earns the most?

Bill and Ellen had just begun work at their first jobs and were talking about them.

"I get paid $18,000 for the first six months," said Ellen. "Then my salary goes up $500 every six months from then on."

"My salary is $36,000 a year," Bill told her. "I get a $2,000 raise at the beginning of each year."

If they both keep working at their jobs for five years, who will earn the most money?

(answer on page 202)

# Squirrels and acorns

Two squirrels named Chatter and Chitter were gathering acorns for winter. They had agreed to divide all the acorns they gathered into two equal shares.

Each squirrel gathered all the acorns he could find. Then the two got together to divide up the acorns. But squirrels are not very good at arithmetic. It took them three tries to divide the acorns equally!

On the first try, Chatter gave Chitter as many acorns as Chitter already had. But that did not make things even, so they tried again.

On the second try, Chitter gave back to Chatter as many acorns as Chatter now had. But that still did not make things even.

On the third try, Chitter gave Chatter 10 more acorns. That made everything right, because now each one had 50 acorns.

How many acorns had each squirrel collected?

(answer on page 203)

# The five hobbyists

In a small town live five ladies who are close friends. Their names are Ms. Schmidt, Ms. Rodriguez, Miss Fujimoto, Mrs. Kowalski, and Mrs. Robinson.

Each lady has a different hobby. One is a gardener. One makes pottery. One knits. One is a painter. One writes stories.

From the following six clues, can you tell which lady has which hobby?

1. Mrs. Kowalski does not care for gardening.

2. The gardener and Ms. Schmidt went to school together.

3. Mrs. Kowalski and Miss Fujimoto wear scarves that were made by the knitter.

4. Miss Fujimoto and the writer often have lunch with the gardener.

5. The gardener, the knitter, and Ms. Rodriguez have some of the vases made by the pottery maker.

6. Mrs. Kowalski asked Ms. Rodriguez if she thought the painter would do a portrait of her daughter.

(answers on page 204)

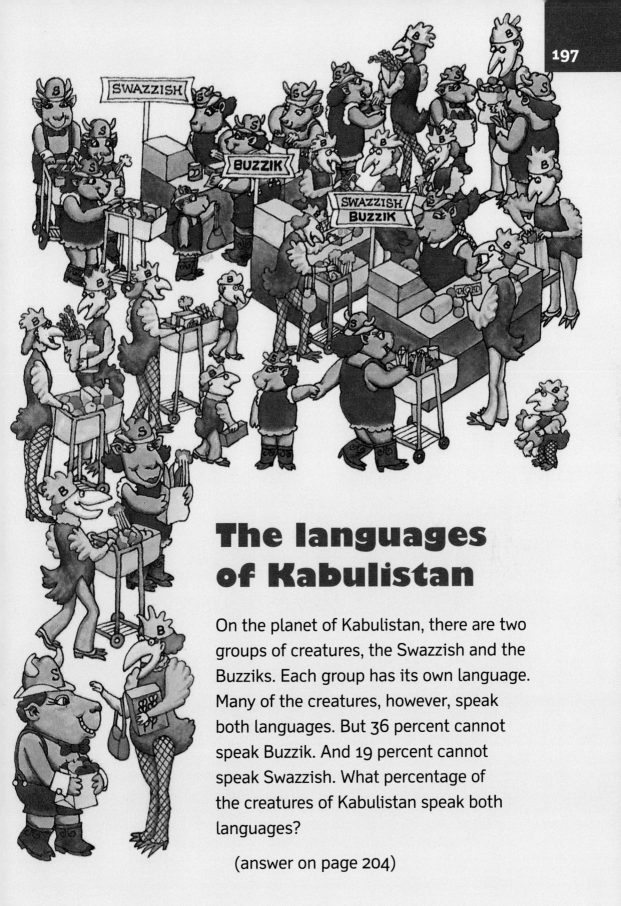

SWAZZISH

BUZZIK

SWAZZISH
BUZZIK

# The languages of Kabulistan

On the planet of Kabulistan, there are two groups of creatures, the Swazzish and the Buzziks. Each group has its own language. Many of the creatures, however, speak both languages. But 36 percent cannot speak Buzzik. And 19 percent cannot speak Swazzish. What percentage of the creatures of Kabulistan speak both languages?

(answer on page 204)

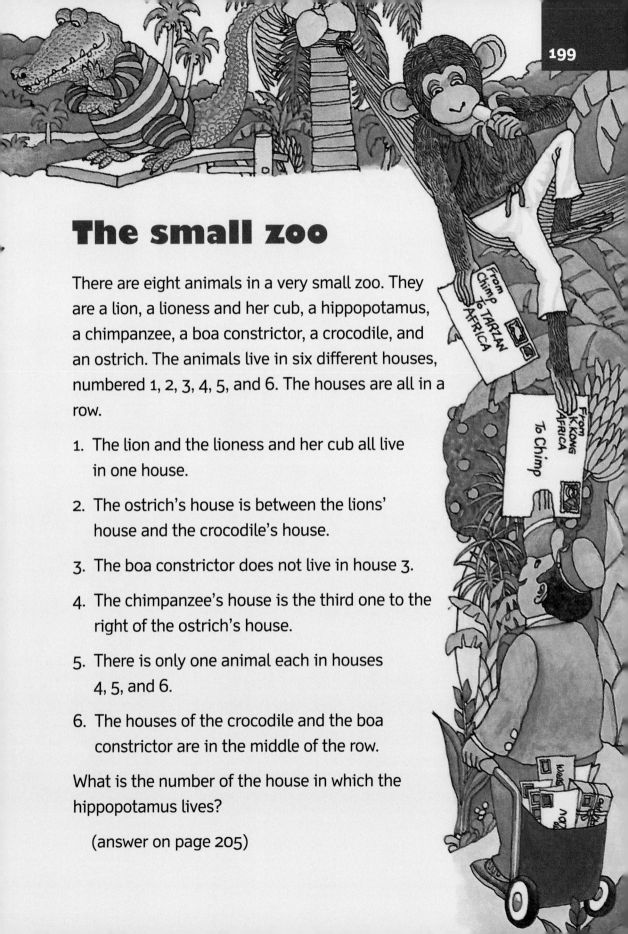

# The small zoo

There are eight animals in a very small zoo. They are a lion, a lioness and her cub, a hippopotamus, a chimpanzee, a boa constrictor, a crocodile, and an ostrich. The animals live in six different houses, numbered 1, 2, 3, 4, 5, and 6. The houses are all in a row.

1.  The lion and the lioness and her cub all live in one house.

2.  The ostrich's house is between the lions' house and the crocodile's house.

3.  The boa constrictor does not live in house 3.

4.  The chimpanzee's house is the third one to the right of the ostrich's house.

5.  There is only one animal each in houses 4, 5, and 6.

6.  The houses of the crocodile and the boa constrictor are in the middle of the row.

What is the number of the house in which the hippopotamus lives?

(answer on page 205)

# The dull movie

A very dull movie was being shown at the Cinema Theater one evening. The movie was so bad that one-third of the audience left during the first part of it. One-half of the rest left during the middle part. And one-half of those left in the theater walked out during the last part. Only 25 people were in their seats when the movie ended.

How many people were in the audience when the movie began?

(answer on page 206)

# The small round table

King Ondolph of Puggia was not as great a king as King Arthur of Britain. Ondolph commanded only six knights—Sir Pudno, Sir Mollix, Sir Baffin, Sir Coddle, Sir Morgid, and Sir Dollop. However, King Ondolph wanted to be as much like King Arthur as possible. So he had a round table built for his knights to sit at. (Of course, it was a rather small round table, for there were only six knights!)

When all six knights sat at the table, the strongest knight was across from Sir Coddle, who was to the right of Sir Baffin. Sir Pudno sat across from the fattest knight, and to the right of the strongest knight. The knight in red armor sat between Sir Coddle and the thin knight, and across from the knight who rode a white horse. And Sir Dollop sat to the right of the left-handed knight, across from the thin knight, and next to Sir Mollix.

From all this, can you figure out:

1. The name of the strongest knight?

2. The name of the knight in red armor?

3. The name of the left-handed knight?

4. The name of the thin knight?

5. The name of the fattest knight?

6. The name of the knight who rode a white horse?

(answers on page 207)

## Who earns the most? (page 194)

It seems as if Bill, with his yearly $2,000 raise should earn more. But Ellen will actually earn $500 a year more than Bill.

Bill gets his raise at the beginning of each year. So, he will not have a raise during his first year. He will just make his $36,000 salary. But Ellen gets a $500 raise after her first six months. She earned $18,000 the first six months, and $18,500 the next six. That's a total of $36,500—which is $500 more than Bill will make.

At the start of his second year, Bill gets a $2,000 raise. He will earn $38,000.

Ellen gets another $500 raise at the end of her second six months of work. So, her salary for the first six months of the second year will go up to $19,000. She gets another raise midway through the year, to $19,500. So, for her second year, she will make $38,500 altogether. Again, that's $500 more than Bill will earn.

Ellen will always be $500 ahead of Bill. At the end of five years, she will have earned $2,500 more than Bill.

## Squirrels and acorns (page 195)

Because the squirrels finished with 50 acorns each, you know, of course, that they started with a total of 100 acorns. To find out how many each squirrel had collected, you work backwards.

On the third try, Chitter gave Chatter 10 acorns and they both had 50. That means that *before* the third try, Chitter must have had 60 acorns and Chatter had 40.

On the second try, Chitter gave Chatter as many acorns as Chatter already had. This left Chitter with 60 and Chatter with 40. So, before this, Chatter must have had 20 acorns and Chitter, 80.

Chitter has the 80 acorns after the first try, when Chatter gave him as many acorns as Chitter already had. So Chitter must have started with 40 acorns, and Chatter gave him 40 more to make 80. And if Chitter started with 40 acorns, Chatter must have started with 60.

## The five hobbyists (page 196)

Clues 1, 2, and 4 tell us that the gardener cannot be Mrs. Kowalski, Ms. Schmidt, or Miss Fujimoto. Clue 5 reveals that Ms. Rodriguez isn't the gardener either. That leaves only Mrs. Robinson. She is the gardener.

Clue 3 tells us that neither Mrs. Kowalski nor Miss Fujimoto is the knitter. Clue 5 also shows that Ms. Rodriguez is not the knitter. So, the only one left who can be the knitter is Ms. Schmidt.

From clue 5 we also know that Ms. Rodriguez is not the pottery maker. Thus, she has to be either the painter or the writer. Clue 4 reveals that Miss Fujimoto is not the writer, so she must be either the painter or pottery maker. As for Mrs. Kowalski, she might be the painter, the writer, or the pottery maker.

But clue 6 reveals that neither Mrs. Kowalski nor Ms. Rodriguez is the painter. Because Ms. Rodriguez has to be either the painter or the writer, she is obviously the writer. With Mrs. Kowalski ruled out as both painter and writer, she must be the pottery maker. That leaves Miss Fujimoto as the painter.

So, the five hobbyists are:

- Mrs. Robinson, gardener
- Ms. Schmidt, knitter
- Ms. Rodriguez, writer
- Mrs. Kowalski, pottery maker
- Miss Fujimoto, painter.

## The languages of Kabulistan (page 197)

We know that 36 percent of the creatures speak only Swazzish. And 19 percent speak only Buzzik. That is 55 percent who speak only one language. This means that 45 percent of the creatures speak both languages.

# The small zoo (page 199)

Clue 2 reveals that the ostrich's house is between two other houses. This means that the house of the ostrich cannot be either house 1 or 6. It has to be 2, 3, 4, or 5.

Clue 3 indicates that the snake lives in house 1, 2, 4, 5, or 6.

Clue 4 says that the chimpanzee's house is the third one from the ostrich's house. The ostrich's house is known to be 2, 3, 4, or 5. But there can't be a third house after house 4 or 5 because that house would be 7 or 8, and there are only 6 houses. So, we know the ostrich lives in 2 or 3. The third house from 2 is 5, and the third from 3 is 6. The chimpanzee must live in 5 or 6.

Up to now, we have learned that:

- The boa constrictor lives in 1, 2, 4, 5, or 6.
- The ostrich lives in 2 or 3.
- The chimpanzee lives in 5 or 6.

Clue 5 reveals there is only one animal each in houses 4, 5, and 6. We know that the lions are together, so they must live in 1, 2, or 3.

Clue 6 tells us the houses of the crocodile and the boa constrictor are in the middle of the row. Thus, they have to be houses 3 and 4, with 1 and 2 on one side, and 5 and 6 on the other. We know from clue 3 that the snake does not live in house 3, so he has to live in house 4. Then the crocodile must live in house 3.

Clue 2 tells us the ostrich's house is between the lions' house and the crocodile's house. We know that the ostrich lives in either house 2 or 3. As the crocodile lives in 3, the ostrich has to live in house 2. Therefore, the lions must live in 1.

The chimpanzee's house is the third one after the ostrich's house. The third house after house 2 is house 5. This leaves only house 6, which has to be the hippo's house.

## The dull movie (page 200)

At the beginning of the movie, there were 150 people in the audience.

To get this answer, you have to work backwards from the number of people that were still in the theater when the movie ended (25).

You know that there were 25 people left after *half* the people walked out during the last part of the movie. As 25 is half of 50, there must have been 50 people in the theater when the last part of the movie began.

You know that half the people in the audience left during the middle part of the movie. Thus, the 50 people still there were the other half. So, there must have been 100 people when the middle part of the movie began.

You know that one-third of the whole audience left during the first part of the movie. Thus, the 100 people who sat through the middle part of the movie were *two-thirds* of the whole audience. If you divide 100 by 2 you will get 50, which is one-third of the *total* audience. Therefore, 50 people left during the first part of the movie, and 50 plus 100 is 150—the number of people in the audience when the movie began.

## The small round table (page 201)

The best way to solve this puzzle is to draw a circle for the table and fill in names and places as the clues reveal them.

The first clue tells us the strongest knight was across from Sir Coddle, who was to the right of Sir Baffin. This gives us three positions.

The second clue says that Sir Pudno sat across from the fattest knight, and to the right of the strongest knight. This gives us two more positions.

Clue three tells us the knight in red armor sat between Sir Coddle and the thin knight. The only person who is between Coddle and someone else is Sir Baffin—so, he is the knight in red armor. And now we also know that as Sir Pudno is on Baffin's other side, he has to be the thin knight.

This clue also gives us the last man at the table, the knight who rode a white horse. And now that everyone is accounted for, we can see that Sir Coddle has to be the left-handed knight.

The last clue tells us that Sir Dollop sat to the right of the left-handed knight. We know that the fattest knight is sitting to the right of Sir Coddle, the left-handed knight, so the fattest knight is Sir Dollop. The clue says that Dollop sat next to Sir Mollix, and as the man to the right of Dollop has been established as the knight who rides a white horse, Mollix is the knight with the white horse.

This leaves only one name unaccounted for—Sir Morgid, who is obviously the strongest knight.

# More Puzzle Books

*Amazing Optical Illusions* by IllusionWorks staff (Firefly Books, 2004)
Thirty optical illusions of different types—photographs, artwork, and computer graphics—try to trick the mind. An explanation accompanies each illusion.

*Can You Find It?* by Judith Cressy (Harry N. Abrams, 2002)

*Can You Find It Too?* by Judith Cressy (Harry N. Abrams, 2004)
In both books, closeup views of famous paintings throughout history and from around the world challenge readers to find the surprises hidden in the details.

*Can You See What I See?* by Walter Wick (Scholastic, 2003- )
Each thematic book in this multivolume set presents photographs that contain hidden objects. Subtitles of the books include *On a Scary, Scary Night* (2008), *Once Upon a Time* (2006), and *Dream Machine* (2003).

*Encyclopedia Brown Cracks the Case* by Donald J. Sobol (Dutton Children's Books, 2007)
Match wits with clever boy-detective Encyclopedia Brown in solving ten crimes, including recovering stolen jewels, retrieving a stuffed tiger, and resolving fake historical "facts."

*Ha! Ha! Ha! And Much More: The Ultimate Round-Up of Jokes, Riddles, Facts, and Puzzles* by Lyn Thomas (Owl Books, 2008)
*Ha! Ha! Ha! 1,000+ Jokes, Riddles, Facts, and More* by Lyn Thomas (Owl Books, 2001)
Hundreds of word puzzles, "Knock! Knock!" jokes, puns, optical illusions, and other ways to have fun with words and pictures are presented, along with background information on how some of them got started.

*I Spy* by Jean Marzollo (Scholastic, 1992- )
Each book in this long-running series contains photographs grouped around a certain subject and having hidden objects that the reader must find. Titles include *I Spy A to Z* (2009), *I Spy a Balloon* (2006), *I Spy a Scary Monster* (2004), and *I Spy a Dinosaur's Eye* (2003).

*Math for All Seasons: Mind Stretching Math Riddles* by Greg Tang (Scholastic, 2002)
*Math Potatoes: Mind Stretching Brain Food* by Greg Tang (Scholastic, 2005)
Clever rhymes help readers learn how to count; add, subtract, multiply, and divide; and solve easy math problems.

*Math Games and Activities from Around the World* by Claudia Zaslavsky (Chicago Review Press, 1998)
*More Math Games and Activities from Around the World* by Claudia Zaslavsky (Chicago Review Press, 2003)
Games and other activities from many different countries teach basic mathematical concepts, all the time showing that math can be fun.

*The Puzzling World of Winston Breen* by Eric Berlin (Putnam Juvenile, 2007)
*The Puzzling World of Winston Breen: The Potato Chip Puzzles* by Eric Berlin (Putnam Juvenile, 2009)
In each book, whiz-kid Winston gets himself involved in a puzzling situation that the reader must try to solve.

*Riddle Me This! Riddles and Stories to Challenge Your Mind* by Hugh Lupton (Barefoot Books, 2003)
Whimsical illustrations give readers clues to solving the riddles and puzzling stories taken from folktales around the world.

*Go Figure!* by Johnny Ball (Dorling Kindersley, 2005)
Color blocks, diagrams, and photo collages combine the history of numbers and number theory, formulas, and mathematical thinking with actual problems to solve.